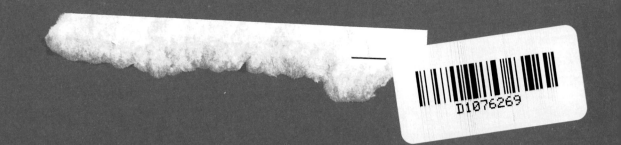

HOME LAB

EXCITING EXPERIMENTS FOR BUDDING SCIENTISTS

Penguin
Random
House

Project art editor Laura Gardner
Project editor Ashwin Khurana
Designer Nicola Erdpresser
Design assistant Sean Ross
Editor Ann Baggaley

Managing editor Lisa Gillespie
Managing art editor Owen Peyton Jones
Producer, pre-production Gillian Reid
Producer Mary Slater
Jacket design development manager Sophia MTT
Managing jackets editor Saloni Singh
Jacket editor Claire Gell
Senior jacket designer Mark Cavanagh
Jacket designer Suhita Dharamjit
Picture researcher Myriam Megharbi

Publisher Andrew Macintyre
Associate publishing director Liz Wheeler
Art director Karen Self
Design director Phil Ormerod
Publishing director Jonathan Metcalf

Writer and consultant Jack Challoner
Photographer Dave King

First published in Great Britain in 2016
by Dorling Kindersley Limited
80 Strand, London, WC2R 0RL

Copyright © 2016 Dorling Kindersley Limited
A Penguin Random House Company
2 4 6 8 10 9 7 5 3 1
001–282970–July/2016

Printed in China

A WORLD OF IDEAS:
SEE ALL THERE IS TO KNOW

www.dk.com

ROBERT WINSTON

HOME LAB

EXCITING EXPERIMENTS FOR BUDDING SCIENTISTS

CONTENTS

FOREWORD

I am often asked what made me want to be a scientist. I was about seven or eight years old when I realized that science was fascinating, and what most interested me was doing my own experiments. I clearly remember the excitement I felt when I realized that I could write secret messages using juice as an invisible ink. Seeing my words appear when I heated paper was something I still find slightly weird and a bit of a thrill.

Making your own invisible ink is just one of the 28 amazing experiments in *Home Lab*. You will also learn how to make different types of paper plane and find out why an object that's heavier than air doesn't just fall to the ground. As a child, I liked to see whether I could get my planes to go further by altering their wings in different ways. You can try this for yourself – or perhaps go the extra mile and figure out how to get your plane to do a loop-the-loop!

All of the experiments in this book are a lot of fun, but it is also important to play it safe. None of the projects is dangerous, but some of them will require an adult's help. For example, you'll use an oven when cooking a baked Alaska, and hot water is needed to make sugar crystal lollipops. It is also important to keep your workplace clean and to wash your hands before and after some experiments, especially if they include food.

Science depends on experimentation – from coders working on Internet security to medical breakthroughs in cancer research. So it may seem surprising that most scientists two thousand years ago preferred to just sit around and discuss their theories. In fact, it is really only in the last four hundred years or so that scientists began to conduct experiments. The pioneering astronomer Galileo Galilei used a telescope to study Jupiter, to count its moons, and record their movements.

In the same way, when you try any of the projects in *Home Lab*, not only will you learn about the world around you, you'll also embark on a scientific journey, just like Galileo – and me! And don't be afraid to make little changes, as that's how science advances. If you have any setbacks, don't see these as failures. They're opportunities to look at the experiment again, using a fresh approach.

I hope you really enjoy this book. And remember, when you try out these experiments you will be exploring some of the very things that made me want to become a scientist.

Robert Winston.

ROBERT WINSTON

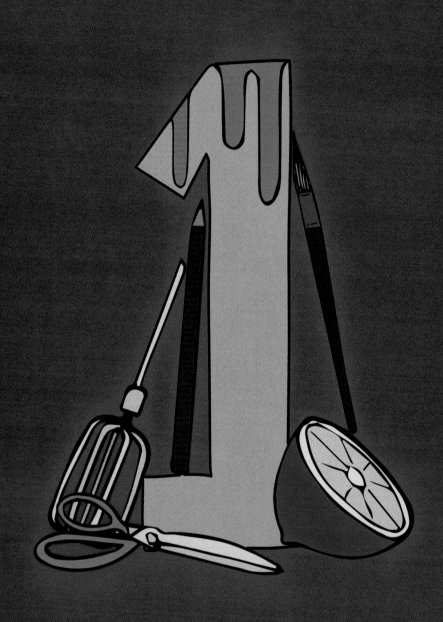

FOOD FOR THOUGHT

The kitchen is a great place to learn about science. The experiments in this chapter use food that could be in your cupboard, fridge, or fruit bowl right now. You'll find out how to grow sparkling crystals, keep food ice-cold in a hot oven, and make electricity. Some experiments produce yummy edible treats you can share with friends, and you'll find plenty of exciting projects to nourish your brain!

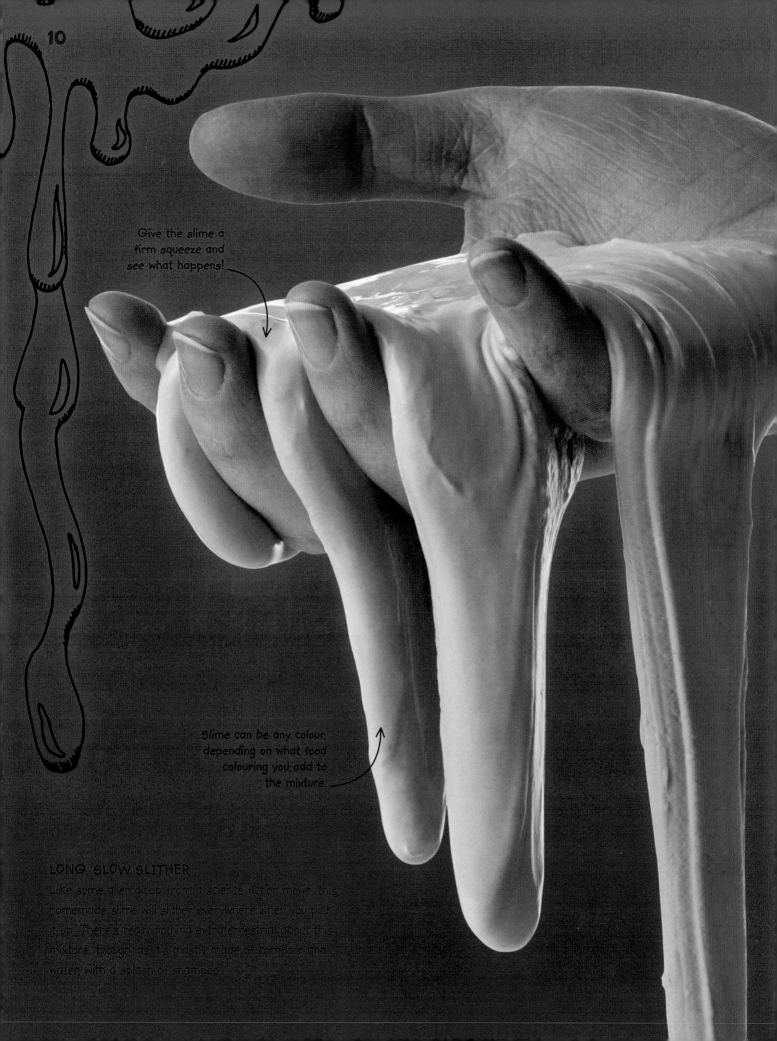

Give the slime a
firm squeeze and
see what happens!

Slime can be any colour,
depending on what food
colouring you add to
the mixture.

LONG, SLOW SLITHER

Like some alien gloop from a science fiction movie, this
homemade slime will slither everywhere when you pick
it up. There's really nothing extraterrestrial about this
mixture, though, as it's mostly made of cornflour and
water, with a splash of shampoo.

STICKY SLIME

This sticky substance is easy to make, fun to play with, and behaves very weirdly indeed. Hold it in your hand for just a few seconds and see if you can figure out if it is a solid or a liquid. Not sure? There's no wonder, as this slime will flow through your fingers like a thick liquid, but then, if you give it a squeeze, it will behave like a solid. Believe it or not, gooey mixtures like this are still liquids even when they're behaving like solids. Try not to make too much of a mess!

HOW TO MAKE
STICKY SLIME

This experiment can get messy, so put down greaseproof paper to catch any sticky spills. Although there's nothing poisonous in the mixture, don't put the slime in your mouth. If you want slime that is more gloopy, warm water is ideal – but don't use boiling water, which could scald you. It's also a good idea to wash your hands after you've finished playing with the slime, as this avoids getting slime all over the furniture!

Time	Difficulty
20 minutes	Medium

WHAT YOU NEED

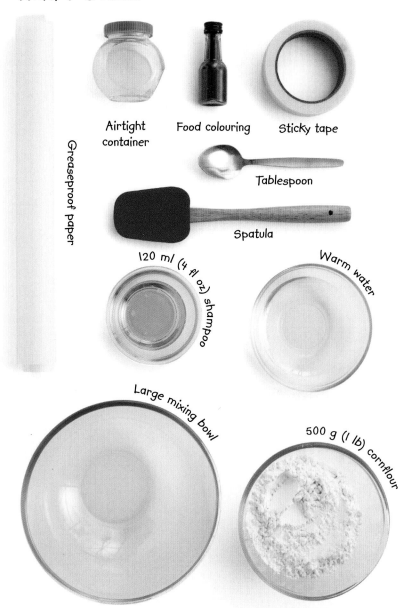

Greaseproof paper

Airtight container

Food colouring

Sticky tape

Tablespoon

Spatula

120 ml (4 fl oz) shampoo

Warm water

Large mixing bowl

500 g (1 lb) cornflour

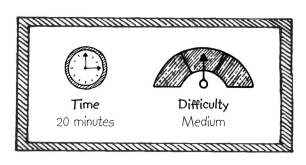

1 Tape a sheet of greaseproof paper to your work surface. Pour a generous amount of food colouring into the large mixing bowl. Then add the shampoo. Notice how slowly the shampoo flows – the technical term for this gloopy behaviour is "viscosity".

2 Add the cornflour to the mixing bowl and stir the contents with the spatula. This is hard at the start because there's a lot of powder and not much liquid. Don't worry: more liquid is going in.

3 Add a few tablespoonfuls of warm water. Keep stirring with your spatula to mix the water into the cornflour. The water makes starch (a substance in the cornflour) expand, forming a network that holds the water and cornflour together in a slimy mixture.

4 Gradually, your mixture will turn into a thick paste. Pick it up and knead it in your hands – it will get really gloopy! But if you thump or *squeeze* the slime, its viscosity increases enormously and it becomes hard, like a solid.

5 Now go for it! Squash, punch, or slam your slime on the table to make it turn solid. Whenever you stop, it will turn into a liquid again. If you want to keep the slime, pour it into an airtight container while it's runny. That way it won't dry out and you can use it for about a month.

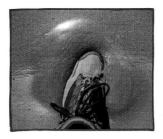

HOW IT WORKS

A molecule is the smallest part of a compound. It's the starch molecules reacting with water that are responsible for the slime's viscosity. As long as the molecules can move around, the mixture stays liquid. Sudden pressure, though, makes the molecules jam together, so the mixture can't flow.

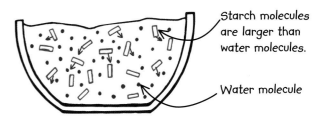

Starch molecules are larger than water molecules.

Water molecule

WITHOUT PRESSURE

As long as you handle the slime gently and don't squish it too hard, the starch molecules can move about, suspended in the water. This makes a thick, slow-flowing liquid.

The starch molecules lock together.

The water molecules are squeezed out.

WITH PRESSURE

If you press hard on the slime, you squeeze out the water molecules from between the starch molecules, which lock together and make the slime feel more solid.

REAL WORLD SCIENCE
QUICKSAND

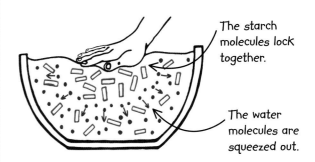

A liquid with a viscosity that changes under pressure is known as a "non-Newtonian fluid". Some of these liquids, such as slime, get thicker and behave like solids. But quicksand – a mixture of sand, clay, and water – is an example of a liquid that gets runnier. If you get stuck in quicksand and struggle to get out, your movements will cause you to sink.

INVISIBLE INK

If you want to write a hidden message or make a treasure map that you want to keep secret, then you need invisible ink. One of the easiest and most effective invisible inks is lemon juice. Write a message on paper with lemon juice, and the message will instantly disappear because the juice dries clear. To reveal the message, apply some heat and watch it appear before your eyes.

Keep your invisible ink in a jar.

Paintbrushes and cotton buds are good tools to use for applying the ink.

Once the paper is heated, the lines on the map appear as dark brown marks.

HIDDEN TREASURE

This map was drawn with lemon juice on white paper. It was invisible before it was put in a hot oven. The heat caused a chemical reaction to take place on the lemon-soaked paper, making the brown colour of the lines appear to reveal the secret map.

HOW TO MAKE
INVISIBLE INK

The ink in this experiment is pure lemon juice. When it dries, it's invisible! To reveal your lemon-juice message or map, you need to put the paper into a hot oven. Find an adult for this part and follow the suggested temperature setting – any hotter may cause the paper to catch fire. If you are using a gas oven, make sure the paper is placed away from the flame.

Time 45 minutes	**Difficulty** Medium	**Warning** Hot oven! Be careful, and get help from an adult

WHAT YOU NEED

Chopping board

White paper

Small bowl

Knife

Lemon

Cotton bud

Oven glove

You will also need an oven

1 Cut the lemon in half and squeeze its juice into the small bowl. Once you've got as much of the juice as you can from the lemon, put its flesh and skin into a composter or recycling bin. Then wash and dry your hands.

2 Dip the cotton bud into the lemon juice and write a message or draw something on the paper. At first, you will be able to see the lines that you draw, but then, as the lemon juice dries on the paper, it will become invisible.

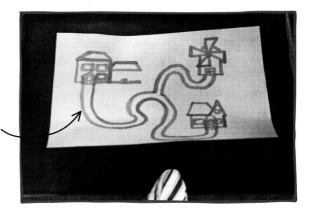

This hidden message was actually a secret map!

3 With the help of an adult, set the oven to 200°C (400°F, gas mark 6). Place your paper on a baking tray and, when the oven is hot enough, use your oven glove to put it inside the oven.

4 After half an hour, your invisible markings should have become visible. With an adult's help, use the oven glove to remove the tray from the oven and put it on a heatproof surface to cool down.

5 Once the tray has cooled, pick up the paper – it will feel brittle. The heat of the oven dried the paper out, and there may be some scorch marks, too, where the paper got extra hot.

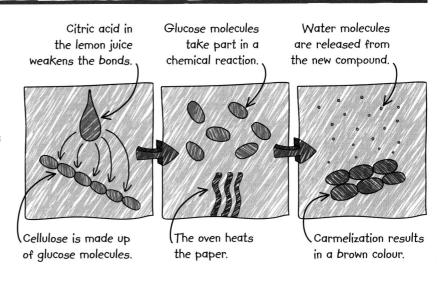

Scorch marks make the paper look old.

It is actually the paper, not the lemon juice, that turns brown.

Paper naturally goes brown with age – **lemon juice and heat** speed up the process.

HOW IT WORKS

Paper is made of a compound called cellulose. Each large molecule of cellulose is made up of thousands of smaller molecules of glucose (a type of sugar) that are bonded together. The citric acid in lemon juice slowly weakens the bonds between the glucose molecules, freeing some of them. When the paper is heated to over 170°C (340°F), these free molecules react together in a chemical process called caramelization. This produces new compounds that have a brown colour and makes the ink visible.

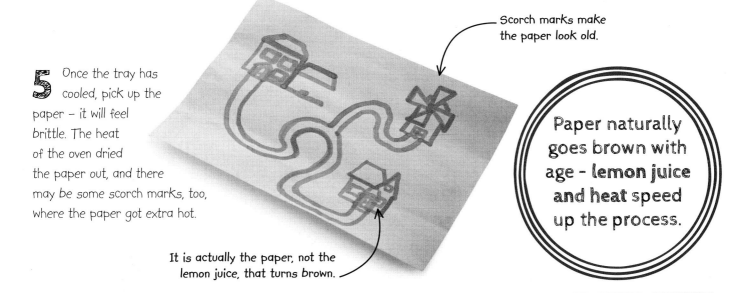

Citric acid in the lemon juice weakens the bonds.

Glucose molecules take part in a chemical reaction.

Water molecules are released from the new compound.

Cellulose is made up of glucose molecules.

The oven heats the paper.

Carmelization results in a brown colour.

BAKED ALASKA

Put ice cream in a hot oven and you'd expect it to melt to slush within a few minutes. Well, that's not what happens when you make *baked Alaska*, a scrumptious dessert that teaches you a great deal about the science of heat transfer. And it tastes great, too. It's not generally a good idea to eat your experiments... but this one is an exception, and it's made for sharing!

IT'S COLD INSIDE

Yes, you really can put ice cream in a hot oven, as long as you surround it with something that does not allow heat to pass through easily. Materials that do that are called insulators. In a baked Alaska, there are two insulators: whisked egg whites and cake.

The oven-baked ice cream hasn't melted!

Light, fluffy meringue is surprisingly heat resistant.

The experiment uses chocolate cake, but you can choose a different flavour if you like.

HOW TO MAKE A
BAKED ALASKA

Making this surprising pud is really straightforward, but you need to be a cook as well as a scientist. This means using kitchen equipment, including a hot oven, so get some help from an adult. You can buy a ready-made cake for the base – or persuade your helpful adult to make one! Before you start, leave the ice cream out of the freezer for about 20 minutes, to soften. And remember – wash your hands before handling food.

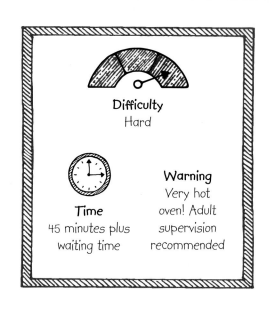

Difficulty
Hard

Time
45 minutes plus waiting time

Warning
Very hot oven! Adult supervision recommended

WHAT YOU NEED

Oven gloves

Small bowl

Four eggs

Clingfilm

Egg cup

Spoon

Glass mixing bowl and pudding bowl

Ice cream

Large and small palette knives

Cream of tartar

Chocolate cake on ovenproof plate

Electric whisk

400 g (14 oz) sugar

You will also need an oven

Don't worry too much about smoothing out creases in the clingfilm.

1 Line the glass pudding bowl with two layers of clingfilm. Make sure you leave plenty of film hanging over the edge of the bowl. You'll need this to hold on to later, when you lift the ice cream you are about to fill the bowl with.

If your ice cream doesn't scoop easily, leave it for a few more minutes.

2 Using a spoon, scoop the ice cream into the bowl to about two thirds of the way up. Press it in with the back of the spoon and smooth the top. Put the bowl in the freezer for at least an hour.

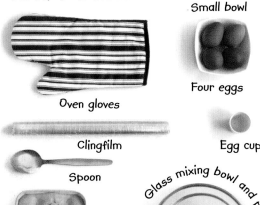

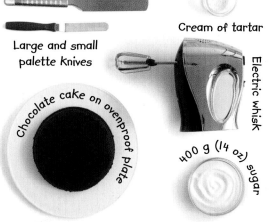

Hold on to the small bowl firmly throughout this process.

3 Preheat the oven to 230°C (450°F, gas mark 8). Then, to start making the meringue, crack an egg into the small bowl. If bits of shell fall in, fish them out – but don't break the yolk!

4 You make meringue with egg whites only. To separate the yolk, place the egg cup over it and pour the white into the mixing bowl. Do the same with the other three eggs. Discard the four yolks.

Don't use the whisk with wet hands, and unplug it when you've finished.

5 Whisk the egg whites on high speed until they are frothy. If you want help with this, ask an adult. Then add ½ teaspoon of cream of tartar. Keep whisking, but stop to test the mixture every few seconds. It's ready when it forms stiff peaks.

6 Now gradually add the sugar to the egg whites and get whisking again. Keep going until the mixture looks shiny and stiff. Then stop and ask an adult to help you remove the whisk blades and clean them.

The mixture should stay in peaks when you lift up the whisk blades.

7 Take the ice cream out of the freezer. Lift it out of its bowl by gently pulling the clingfilm. Turn it upside down on top of the cake, ensuring it doesn't overlap the edge. Carefully peel away the clingfilm.

Cover every part of the ice cream and cake with the meringue mixture, leaving no gaps.

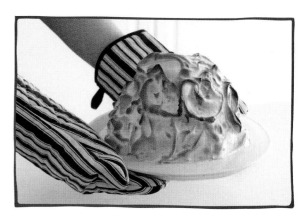

8 This is where you have to be extra quick and careful! With the help of an adult, use the spatula to spread the meringue all over the ice cream and the cake. Then, using oven gloves, put the plate into the hot oven and cook the pud for three minutes – or until the outside browns.

9 Your baked Alaska is ready to come out of the oven and it looks wonderful. The plate will be very hot, so use oven gloves (and maybe some adult help) to lift out the plate and put it on a heat-resistant surface. Now, here's the hard bit – let your pud stand for a minute or so before serving it!

The meringue is very hot when it's taken out of the oven.

The ice cream is still cold!

The cake slowed down the heat transfer from the hot plate to the ice cream.

10 This is the moment you've been waiting for! Cut open the baked Alaska. You should find that, amazingly, the ice cream is still solid and cold – despite having been in a very hot oven. There's too much for one person to eat, so why not invite friends and family to share the treat?

TAKE IT FURTHER

Try making mini baked Alaskas, using biscuits instead of cake. Since biscuits are thinner than cake, and you will probably apply a thinner layer of whisked egg whites, the ice cream will be less well insulated against the hot air inside the oven. However, it will take less time to cook the egg whites, so you can reduce the amount of time you cook the pudding for – and hopefully, your ice cream will still not have melted.

HOW IT WORKS

Egg white is mostly water with a little sugar dissolved in it plus long molecules of protein (mostly one called albumin). In their natural state, albumin molecules are coiled up. But when you whisk egg whites, the molecules uncoil. These then join together, trapping tiny pockets of air in between them. Air is a good heat insulator, which means that heat passes through it very slowly. So while the surface of your baked Alaska cooks quickly, the heat takes much longer to pass right through the trapped air to the ice cream.

This dessert is named after the American state of Alaska, where it gets very cold.

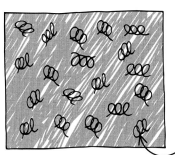

 Air bubbles are formed.

A stiff foam is created.

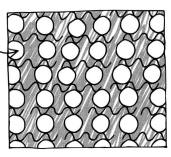

The long molecules of albumin are coiled up.

Albumin molecules start to link up.

Egg white is 90 per cent water and 10 per cent protein. It's the proteins that make egg white gloopy.

Whisking egg whites unwinds the albumin molecules and introduces millions of tiny air bubbles.

The albumin molecules join up, trapping the air bubbles. When the foam is cooked, it hardens and browns – it's a meringue!

REAL WORLD SCIENCE
INCREDIBLE IGLOOS

Like whisked egg whites, snow contains lots of trapped air, and is a very good insulator. That's why people can stay warm in an igloo, a shelter made from bricks of snow and traditionally built by communities living in northern Canada and Greenland.

KEEPING WARM

Body heat warms the air inside an igloo, and the snow slows down heat loss. Igloos, now used mostly by explorers and mountaineers, can save lives in snowstorms.

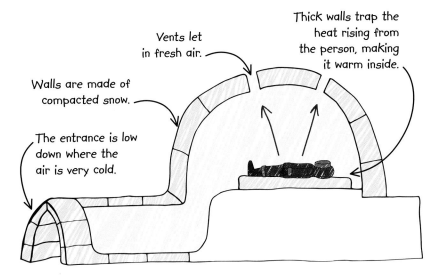

Thick walls trap the heat rising from the person, making it warm inside.

Vents let in fresh air.

Walls are made of compacted snow.

The entrance is low down where the air is very cold.

MONSTER MARSHMALLOWS

Something *big* is happening in the kitchen. If you like marshmallows, you'll love this experiment because it turns those delicious gooey sweets into jumbo-sized treats. Before your very eyes, they will puff up like bread or cakes rising in the oven – but much, much faster. All it takes is a microwave oven and about half a minute. The results are so good you might just want to do the experiment again and again. Buy a bag of marshmallows and prepare to be astonished!

Sweets are allowed in the lab for this experiment!

Get a range of colours, if you can.

A LOT OF HOT AIR

There's nothing spooky about these monster marshmallows. The reason they puff up, or expand, is because they contain lots of air. If you keep repeating the experiment, don't forget that every time a marshmallow comes out of the microwave it will be extremely hot and sticky.

Marshmallows swell up incredibly fast when heated.

The plate turns in the microwave so the marshmallow is heated evenly.

HOW TO MAKE
MONSTER MARSHMALLOWS

This experiment is really quick, simple, and fun. You just need a microwave oven, some marshmallows, and a microwave-safe plate. Don't heat the marshmallows for too long – they will turn brown, and may not taste nice. Before scoffing your sticky treat, let the marshmallows stand for a minute or so after you take them out of the microwave. They will be very hot and could scald your mouth.

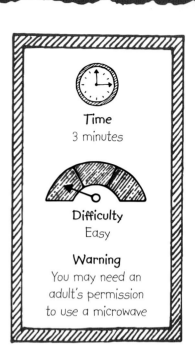

Time
3 minutes

Difficulty
Easy

Warning
You may need an adult's permission to use a microwave

WHAT YOU NEED

Marshmallows on
a microwave-safe plate

You will also need
a microwave oven

1 Place a marshmallow on the plate, and put the plate in the microwave. Microwaves are a form of invisible radiation that can heat certain things, like marshmallows, very quickly.

2 Close the microwave door, set the timer for 30 seconds, and press "start". The powerful rays produced by the microwave bounce around and hit the marshmallow, which absorbs their energy.

3 Stand back and watch carefully through the microwave door. After about 15 seconds, your marshmallow should begin to increase in size!

4 When the time is up, remove the plate carefully – the marshmallow will be hot! Repeat the experiment for one minute: what do you think will happen?

TAKE IT FURTHER

Try this quick and sticky test. Take care though, as the marshmallows can get very hot. You may want an adult at hand to help out, just in case.

1 Grab a handful of mini marshmallows and assemble a little pyramid on a microwave-safe plate. Take some time perfecting your structure.

The marshmallows expand quickly, taking up most of the plate!

2 Set the microwave timer for a 30 second blast. Watch the marshmallows combine with each other, as they slump into a bubbling, pillowy mass.

Before your very eyes, the marshmallows will flatten to almost nothing.

3 OK, are you ready to see something cool? Set the microwave timer for another 30 seconds. What have you got now? A plate of very sticky, hot liquid!

HOW IT WORKS

A marshmallow has a foamy, squashy texture *because it has thousands* of tiny air pockets inside it. Gases, such as air, are made of molecules moving freely at high speed and bouncing off any surfaces they meet. As they bounce, the molecules put pressure on the surfaces. Heating a gas causes the molecules to move faster, which increases the pressure. When you heat a marshmallow, each tiny air pocket blows up like a balloon.

As the air heats up, the pressure it exerts increases and the pockets grow bigger.

A marshmallow contains lots of tiny air pockets.

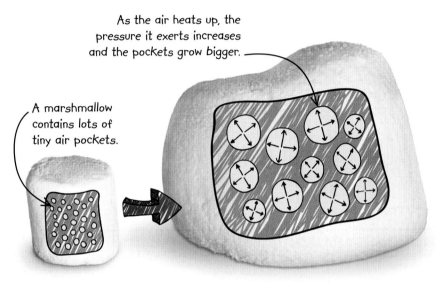

The air *bubbles inside an* uncooked marshmallow are small and stable.

Very quickly, the air inside expands, pushing against the marshmallow's soft, sugary walls.

REAL WORLD SCIENCE
MELT IN THE MOUTH

A thickener called gelatin that is inside a marshmallow melts at a temperature just *below that* of the human *body*: 37°C (98.6°F). That is why marshmallows "melt in your mouth". The low melting temperature is important in your experiment *because* marshmallows become soft as they heat up, which makes it easier for them to expand. Another sweet that melts in the mouth is chocolate. The makers of chocolate carefully adjust their recipes to ensure that their products spread easily across your tongue.

SUGAR CRYSTAL LOLLIPOPS

Would you *believe* that you can actually grow your own lollipops? In this fun experiment, you will make colourful treats that not only look *beautiful* but taste delicious. These lollipops form as trillions of tiny sugar molecules stick together and grow into glittering crystals. They can sometimes take a week to get big enough to eat, but it's worth the wait.

SPECIAL TREATS

Eating too much sugar is *bad* for our health and can damage your teeth, but it's fine to have a treat just every now and then. These lollipops are flavoured naturally with a tang of lemon. You can also colour them using food colouring made with natural ingredients.

Large sugar crystals take at least several days to grow.

A barbecue skewer makes a great lollipop stick.

Use different food colourings to really give your lollipops a sparkle.

HOW TO MAKE
SUGAR CRYSTAL LOLLIPOPS

This experiment isn't complicated, but it needs a bit of patience as your lollipops will take at least a few days to "grow". You'll need to handle a pan of nearly boiling syrupy solution, so find an adult who can help you before you start. If you find measuring out the ingredients a bit tricky, you can ask an adult to help you with this bit, too. You should be able to make several lolllipops from one batch of solution.

Time
20 minutes plus up to a week for growth

Difficulty
Medium

Warning
An adult is vital, as this experiment includes the use of a hob and hot water

WHAT YOU NEED

1 kg (35 oz) sugar

Narrow glass (one per lollipop)

Kitchen towel

Food colouring

Wooden skewer

Spatula

Lemon

Peg

Saucepan filled with 200 g (7 fl oz) of cold water

You will also need a hob

Take care with this pour and you'll avoid making a big mess!

The rings on the hob get hot, so get a responsible adult to help you.

1 Your amazing crystals will grow out of a strong sugar solution. So you first need to mix lots of sugar into some water. Put the saucepan filled with 200 ml (7 fl oz) of water onto a hob and add 800 g (28 oz) of the sugar. With the help of an adult, turn on the hob to high.

2 As the water gets hotter, use your spatula to gently stir the mixture, but watch out for hot splashes! If you are nervous, ask an adult to help with this part. Soon the sugar will begin to disappear, but keep on stirring.

3 Heat the sugary water for around three minutes. You want the water to be very hot, but not boiling; if bubbles rise to the water's surface, turn down the heat. After a few minutes, you should have a syrupy liquid. Turn off the heat.

4 While your solution cools down, add some food colouring to it. Around 10 drops is enough, so drip it in slowly and carefully. Slice the lemon in half and squeeze a little of the juice into the mixture, to add a zingy flavour. Stir again.

You can make **several lollipops** with this amount of liquid.

The sugar granules provide a perfect surface for the crystals to grow on.

5 Meanwhile, wet one half of a wooden skewer under a tap, then plunge it into the remaining sugar. This leaves a coating of sugar granules clinging to the skewer that will help your crystals to grow. You will need one skewer for every lollipop.

6 After 10 minutes, the solution should be cool enough to pour into your glass. Wait longer if you're not sure, as very hot liquid could crack the glass. If you want to make more than one lollipop, add small amounts of solution to more glasses.

7 Put the skewer into the solution, sugary end first, and hold it in place with a clothes peg. Don't let the skewer touch the bottom. Almost at once, sugar molecules from the solution will begin sticking to the sugar granules.

8 Your solution should stay fresh for a while, as bacteria and other nasties are unlikely to survive in such a sugary liquid. But to keep out dust or insects, you can cover the glass with a piece of kitchen towel pushed down over the skewer.

9 Leave your glass for several days in a safe place. Check each day to see how the sugar crystals are growing. If a sugar crust grows on top of the solution, gently break this and remove it – this will help the lollipop to continue growing.

10 Once your lollipop is large enough, remove the skewer from the solution. Leave the stick to dry – and then enjoy the taste of your own sugar crystal lollipop. Of course, you could always wrap it and give it as a gift.

Keep your fully formed lollipops covered or in the fridge, so they stay fresh.

TAKE IT FURTHER

Instead of edible treats, you can also make exciting decorations using this same sugar-water solution, but without any food colouring. Colourful pipe cleaners have a furry texture that is a good surface for crystals to form on, and they can be bent into fun shapes!

HOW IT WORKS

Each granule of sugar is a tiny crystal made of trillions of sugar molecules held together in a regular pattern. When you mix sugar with water, the sugar molecules break apart to mix among the water molecules, forming a solution. There is a high concentration of sugar molecules in the strong solution you made for this experiment. The concentration increases gradually, as the water evaporates from the surface of the solution. All of the molecules in the solution are slowly moving around, and when the sugar molecules collide with the sugar granules coating the skewer, they may stick. As more and more stick, the crystals grow – and so does your lollipop.

Sugar forms monoclinic crystals

Peg

Wooden skewer

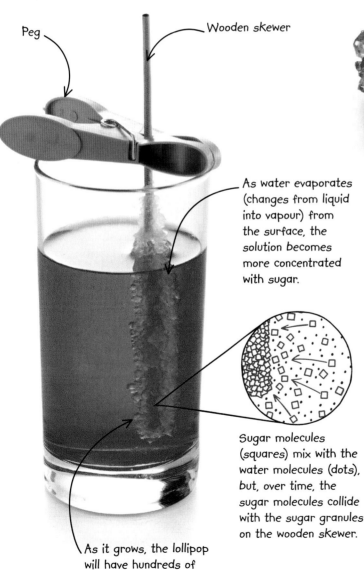

As water evaporates (changes from liquid into vapour) from the surface, the solution becomes more concentrated with sugar.

Sugar molecules (squares) mix with the water molecules (dots), but, over time, the sugar molecules collide with the sugar granules on the wooden skewer.

As it grows, the lollipop will have hundreds of individual crystals.

CRYSTAL SHAPES

The way molecules join together determines the shape of the crystals. The shape of crystals that make up your lollipop is described as "monoclinic", where each crystal has three unequal sides.

REAL WORLD SCIENCE
HOAR FROST

In the same way that sugar molecules mixed with water molecules in this experiment, so too do water molecules mix with oxygen molecules in air. In cold weather, water molecules may join up, forming an icy coating called hoar frost, which clings to surfaces.

LEMON BATTERY

Did you know that you can make a battery using lemons? With just five lemons, some coins, screws, and leads, you can make an electric current flow around a circuit with enough energy to illuminate a small lamp called a light emitting diode (LED). Now just imagine what you could power with one hundred lemons!

Coins are coated with a metal called copper.

Screws are coated with a metal called zinc.

Leads have metal wires inside and connect the coins with the screws.

CELLS, VOLTAGE, AND BATTERIES

One lemon with a coin and a screw in it is one "cell". A single cell produces some electricity, but not with enough energy to light an LED. Energy is measured in volts (V), and a single lemon cell produces about 0.8V. To produce a high enough voltage to light the LED, you need to join five lemon cells together. Multiple cells joined together are called a battery.

LEDs are found in all sorts of electronic equipment.

HOW TO MAKE A
LEMON BATTERY

Ask an adult to help you get hold of what you need. The screws must be galvanized, which means coated with zinc. LEDs and leads with crocodile clips can be found in craft or electronics shops. While this experiment is safe, do remember that electricity can be dangerous. And discard the lemons when you have finished the experiment – don't use them for food.

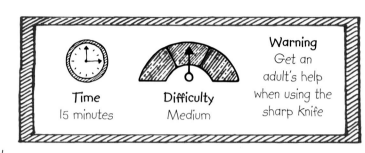

Time
15 minutes

Difficulty
Medium

Warning
Get an adult's help when using the sharp knife

WHAT YOU NEED

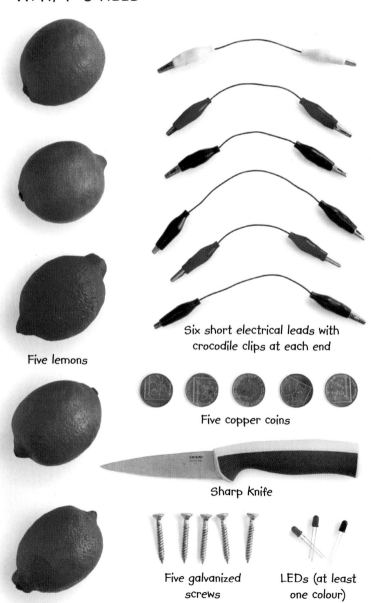

Five lemons

Six short electrical leads with crocodile clips at each end

Five copper coins

Sharp knife

Five galvanized screws

LEDs (at least one colour)

1 With an adult's help, use the knife to make a cut in a lemon, about 1 cm (½ in) from the centre, and roughly 2 cm (¾ in) deep. Now push a coin firmly into the slit you have created. Do the same with the other four lemons.

2 About 1 cm (½ in) from the centre of the first lemon – on the other side to the coin – insert a galvanized screw. Twist it in, clockwise, to secure it in the lemon's flesh. Now repeat with the other four lemons, then arrange the lemons in a circle.

The leads from the first and last lemons both have one end unconnected.

3 Squeeze the crocodile clip on one lead so that it opens, like a crocodile's jaws. Place it around the screw in one lemon, so it grips it. Connect the other clip to the coin in another lemon.

4 Connect all the lemons – coin to screw – as in step 3. For the last lemon, attach a lead to its coin, but don't connect it to the screw in your first lemon. Instead, attach another lead to that screw.

If the light from the LED is weak, try pushing in or wiggling the screws and coins.

5 Each LED has two legs, which are slightly different lengths. With the free end of the lead that is attached to the coin, fix the crocodile clip to the slightly longer leg of the LED.

6 Now connect the crocodile clip of the other free lead that is connected to the screw to the other, shorter leg of the LED. This now completes the circuit to make the LED light up.

HOW IT WORKS

The electric current that lights your LED is actually caused by countless tiny particles called electrons moving around the circuit. Electrons are present inside every atom. As the zinc dissolves in the lemon juice, two electrons are released from each atom of zinc (from the screw). All electrons are negatively charged, and they push apart as they move inside the wire. When they reach the copper coin, they take part in another chemical reaction, allowing electrons to continue flowing around the circuit.

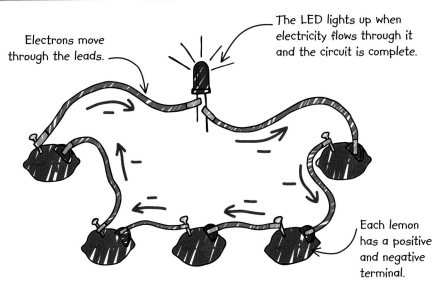

Electrons move through the leads.

The LED lights up when electricity flows through it and the circuit is complete.

Each lemon has a positive and negative terminal.

AROUND THE HOME

It's amazing what experiments you can carry out with everyday items like paper, rubber bands, and balloons. As you'll see in this exciting chapter, you don't need any special materials to understand the structure of DNA or to find out about the planets in our Solar System. There are also experiments with paper planes and static electricity. You'll find most of your equipment somewhere at home – perhaps on your desk or even in the wastepaper basket!

DNA MODEL

This twisting multi-coloured ladder is a model of a very important part of your body – but it's about 10 million times bigger than the real thing! DNA is a tiny molecule with a long name: the initials stand for deoxyribonucleic acid. It is found in all living things on Earth. Every one of the trillions of cells that make up you contains a DNA molecule. Each molecule is a mini database, packed with instructions telling your body how to work properly. You can make an extraordinary DNA model with ordinary items, such as paper, scissors, and coloured highlighters. So let's get snipping!

SPIRAL OF COLOUR

DNA doesn't really come in wacky fluorescent shades, but using these colours makes everything easier to understand. The instructions on the following pages tell you how to arrange the different colours in your DNA model. It's easy and a lot of fun.

Choose fluorescent colours for a really striking effect!

A snazzy DNA spiral would look good decorating your bedroom.

Use tape to fix the rungs of the ladder in place.

HOW TO MAKE A
DNA MODEL

Your finished model of DNA will have a shape like a twisted rope ladder – just like real DNA. It's important to use four different colours when you make the "rungs" of the ladder, because each colour represents one of four different chemicals. You use tape for the "ropes" at the sides of the ladder, which in real DNA are also types of chemicals.

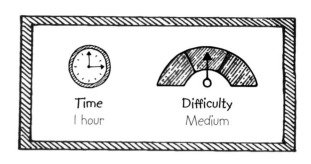

Time
1 hour

Difficulty
Medium

WHAT YOU NEED

Highlighter pens in four different colours

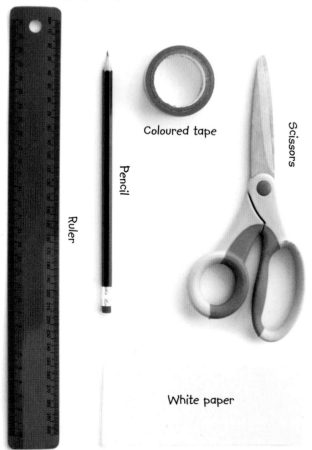

Ruler

Pencil

Coloured tape

Scissors

White paper

1 With a pencil and ruler, mark the paper into about 30 strips, each 1 cm (⅓ in) wide and 3 cm (1¼ in) long. Cut out the strips with scissors. These are the rungs of the ladder and each one represents a pair of chemicals known as "bases".

2 Take each strip and pinch a crease halfway along its length. The crease marks the dividing line between two bases. In real DNA, the two bases in each rung are held together by a chemical bond.

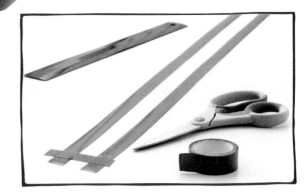

3 Now colour your paper rungs on both sides. One half should be one colour, the other half another. The colours should always be in pairs - for example, yellow always goes with orange.

4 Now cut two strips of tape about 70 cm (28 in) long. Lay the strips face up next to each other, with a gap of 2 cm (¾ in) between them. Stick down the ends with small pieces of the same tape.

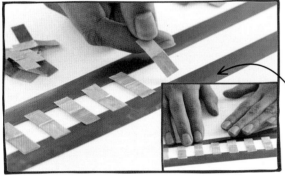

Everybody's DNA is different, so there is no right or wrong combination.

Hold and twist the ladder very carefully.

The paired spiral shape of DNA is called a double helix.

5 Press the coloured rungs, in any order, onto the two lengths of tape, leaving a gap of about 1 cm (⅓ in) between them. When you've used up all the rungs, carefully fold both lengths of sticky tape over them to hold them in place.

6 There's just one more thing to do to make your model perfect: you have to twist the ladder into a spiral shape that's just like DNA itself. Do this very gently to get the twist right, turning the end nearest to you in an anti-clockwise direction.

HOW IT WORKS

The bases in DNA - as represented in the model you created - are a code of instructions for how to make proteins. These are large, complex molecules required for the structure, function, and regulation of the body's tissues and organs. For example, the protein keratin makes up your hair and nails. A section of the DNA ladder that carries a recipe for a particular protein is called a gene. Your entire DNA code consists of about 20,000 genes. Together, your full set of genes is called a genome. No-one else has exactly the same genome as you - unless you have an identical twin.

REAL WORLD SCIENCE
DNA SEQUENCE

Using special equipment, scientists can work out what they call a DNA sequence: the exact arrangement of the bases along the length of a DNA molecule. This means samples can be used to identify people or to spot genes that can cause diseases.

UP, UP, AND AWAY!

The three planes that you will create each behave differently from one another because of the way the air moves around them as they fly. Try out various ways of launching your planes – upwards, downwards, harder, and softer – and experiment by changing the shapes of the wings.

The Super Stunt Plane can do tricks!

The Graceful Glider is designed to stay in the air for a long time.

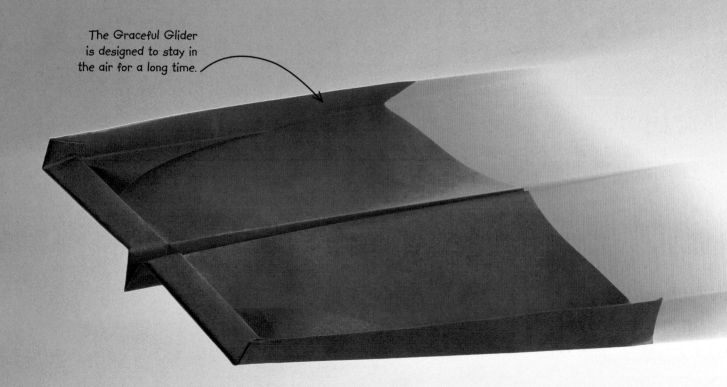

The Dashing Dart is designed for speed and distance.

PAPER PLANES

Drop a piece of paper and it will tumble to the ground, as air escapes chaotically around the flapping sides. With a few folds, a few cuts, and a little know-how, you can make that piece of paper dash along at high speed, glide gracefully, or make impressive manoeuvres, as it flies through the air. In this experiment, you'll be testing out "aerodynamics" – the interaction between the air and objects moving through it. Let's get ready for take-off!

HOW TO MAKE
PAPER PLANES

These three paper planes – an easy, a medium, and a hard one – are fun to make, but follow the instructions carefully for good results. All you really need is paper, but one of the designs requires a ruler, scissors, and tape. Be careful, though, as the Dashing Dart has a sharp nose, so don't throw it towards anyone's face.

WHAT YOU NEED

A4 paper

Ruler

Scissors

Sticky tape

DASHING DART

Built for speed, this simple, streamlined plane zips through the air. When you've made it, throw it at a slight upwards angle – and watch it fly!

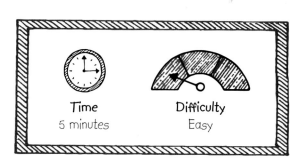

Time
5 minutes

Difficulty
Easy

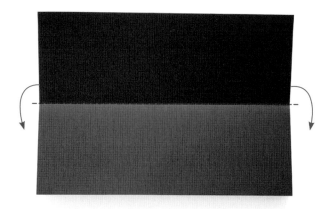

1 Fold a piece of paper in half lengthways as accurately as you can. Make a crease with a fingernail or ruler, then unfold the paper again.

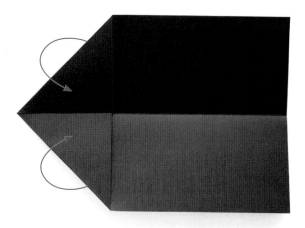

2 Fold down two corners so they meet at the centre line. Leave a small gap between them, otherwise it will be difficult to fold the paper again.

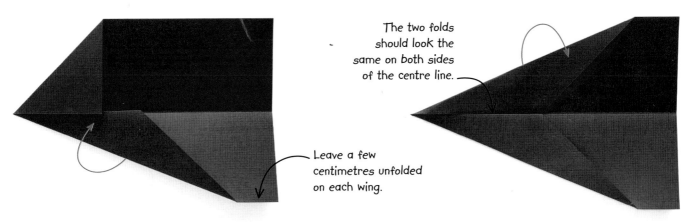

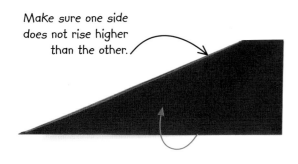

The two folds should look the same on both sides of the centre line.

Leave a few centimetres unfolded on each wing.

3 Now fold down one edge towards the centre line. Again, don't fold it right onto the centre line, as you will soon have to fold the paper lengthways.

4 Do the same with the other edge, making sure the folds are symmetrical and meet close to the line. Check that all your folds are creased.

Make sure one side does not rise higher than the other.

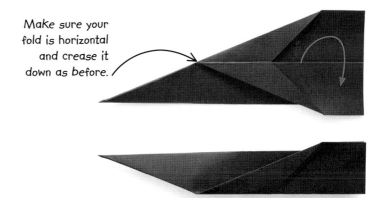

Make sure your fold is horizontal and crease it down as before.

5 Now fold the paper in half lengthways, with the folded sections on the inside. The two sides should match up perfectly. Crease all the folds firmly.

6 Fold down one side, making the fold parallel with the bottom of the plane and about halfway up the back, or tail. Now do the same to the other side.

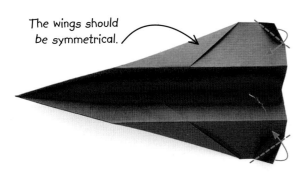

The wings should be symmetrical.

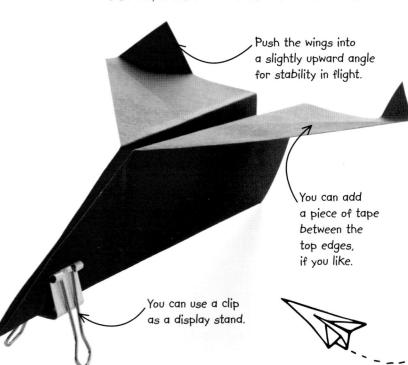

Push the wings into a slightly upward angle for stability in flight.

You can add a piece of tape between the top edges, if you like.

7 Nearly there! Fold up the corners – these will push air upwards as the plane flies, and that will nudge the tail down and the nose up.

You can use a clip as a display stand.

GRACEFUL GLIDER

Launch this plane gently – only slightly above horizontal – and it should glide through the air, staying aloft for longer than the Dashing Dart. But be patient, it's a little fiddly to make.

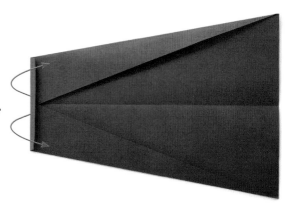

Time	**Difficulty**
10 minutes	Medium

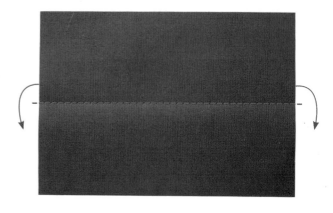

1 Start by carefully folding a piece of paper in half lengthways. Make a crease with a fingernail or ruler, then unfold the paper again.

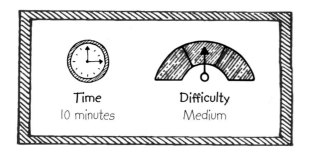

2 Fold in both edges, so that each corner of what will be the front touches the centre line. Both folds should meet at the back corners.

This area should be the same shape on either side of the centre line.

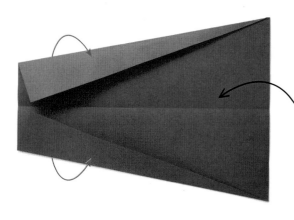

3 Fold down about 1 cm (½ in) of the tapered end of the paper. This will be the nose of the glider. Crease down the fold firmly.

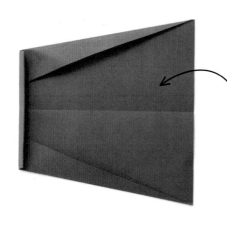

The plane will be noticeably shorter now, but that will help it glide.

4 Repeat step 3 six times, each fold over the last. The folded edges of what will be the wings will buckle, so keep pushing them under the folds.

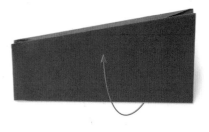

5 Now carefully fold the plane in half, making it as symmetrical as you can. Crease the fold well, especially around the bulky nose of the plane.

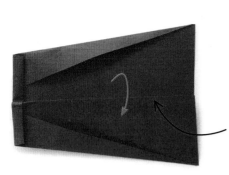

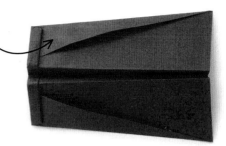

Tuck any ruffled up pieces under the fold as best as you can.

Try to make this line straight.

6 Fold down one side, about 2 cm (¾ in) from the bottom. Once again, crease the fold well, especially at the nose, where the paper is chunky.

7 Do the same to other side, and make sure all of your folds are creased and that the glider is symmetrical. You now have two wings.

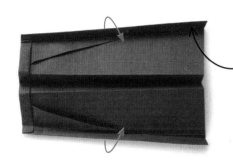

Make these flaps look the same on both wings.

8 Finally, fold along the edges of the wings, making the edges parallel with the centre line. Crease and lift them up, so they stand up vertically.

Experts launch **paper planes** that stay airborne indoors for **30 seconds!**

After each launch, you may need to adjust these flaps, so they remain vertical.

Use a small piece of tape to hold the two sides of the glider together, if you like.

These folds add weight to the nose, keeping the plane balanced in flight.

Use a clip to stand up the glider on display when you are not using it.

SUPER STUNT PLANE

This plane has two flaps and a rudder. By changing the positions of these control surfaces, you can make the plane twist, climb, dive, and even loop-the-loop.

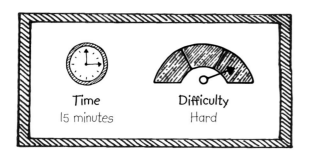

Time
15 minutes

Difficulty
Hard

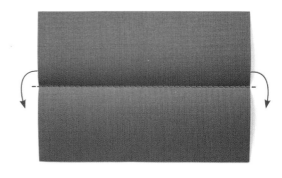

1 Begin by simply folding a piece of paper in half lengthways. Make a crease with a fingernail or ruler, then unfold the paper again.

2 Fold one corner and make a firm crease. Then fold the sharply pointed corner, so you end up with a triangle. Tape around the open diagonal edge.

3 Fold back the point of the triangle, so that it meets the long base of the triangle. Now fold the paper around the centre fold and crease it.

Take this opportunity to crease all of the other folds.

The plane should be symmetrical on both sides of the centre fold.

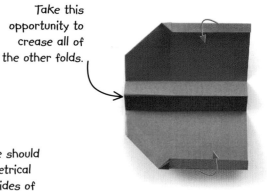

4 For the wings, fold down one side, about 2 cm (¾ in) from the centre fold. Do the same with the other side, and unfold both so that they lie flat.

5 Turn over the plane and fold down the edge of each wing 1 cm (½ in) in from the edge. Lift up both edges, so they sit at right angles to the surface.

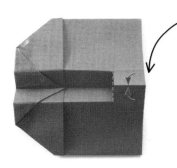

Pinch the tailfin at the top, to ensure a smooth crease.

6 Cut from the centre fold up to the base of the wings – about 2.5 cm (1 in) in from the back of the plane – then push it up. This is the tailfin.

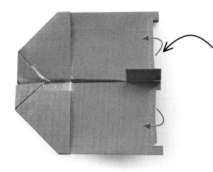

Try to make both slits on either side of the tailfin the same size.

7 Crease the tailfin so it stands up, taping the wings to keep it closed. Cut slits into the trailing edge of each wing and fold up the resulting flaps.

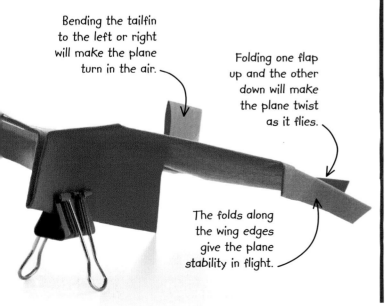

Bending the tailfin to the left or right will make the plane turn in the air.

Folding one flap up and the other down will make the plane twist as it flies.

The folds along the wing edges give the plane stability in flight.

HOW IT WORKS

Flying objects experience four types of force: gravity, lift, thrust, and drag. The Dashing Dart speeds through the air because air passes around its streamlined shape easily without exerting much drag. The Graceful Glider experiences lots of lift because its wings have a large area – so it stays in the air for longer. The control surfaces at the back of the Super Stunt Plane change the airflow, creating lift forces that can act sideways or even downwards, allowing the plane to change direction, or even spin.

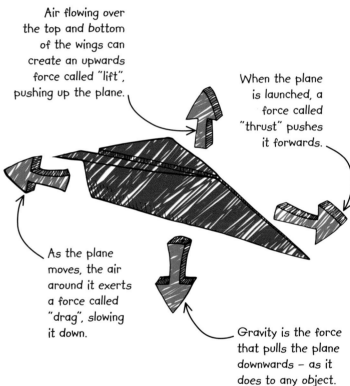

Air flowing over the top and bottom of the wings can create an upwards force called "lift", pushing up the plane.

When the plane is launched, a force called "thrust" pushes it forwards.

As the plane moves, the air around it exerts a force called "drag", slowing it down.

Gravity is the force that pulls the plane downwards – as it does to any object.

REAL WORLD SCIENCE
HANG GLIDER

In the right conditions, with warm air rising up from the ground, a hang glider can stay up for hours. The rising air, called a thermal, pushes up on the underside of the wings, providing lift. To steer, the pilot shifts his or her body to tilt the glider.

SENSATIONAL SPEAKERS

Do you love listening to music on a phone but find it doesn't sound as good as you'd like it to? Maybe your family grumbles every time you play your favourite songs really loud? These terrific smartphone speakers could be the answer to both problems. They not only help to get rid of that "tinny" effect but also direct most of the sound straight to your ears. So your music sounds bigger and better without annoying everyone else in the room.

You can change the colours of your speakers as often as you like.

These brilliant speakers are made from everyday household items.

LOOKS GOOD, SOUNDS EVEN BETTER

Portable mobile phone speakers painted in funky colours look great sitting on your desk or bedside table. They don't even need batteries or recharging. So what are you waiting for? Make some speakers and get a playlist going! But remember, never put the speakers right next to your ears with music at full blast. This could damage your hearing.

Built-in mini loudspeakers are usually located at the bottom of a phone.

HOW TO MAKE
SENSATIONAL SPEAKERS

It's really easy to make these impressive speakers. Just find a cardboard tube and some paper cups, and you're almost there. You will also need scissors to cut some materials, so ask an adult if you need a hand with this part. When you're done, your new speakers will make your music louder and clearer – and, best of all, they won't cost you any pocket money!

Time
20 minutes plus time
for paint to dry

Difficulty
Medium

WHAT YOU NEED

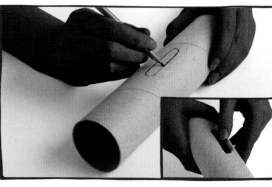

Paints

Mobile phone

Two paper cups

Cardboard tube

Kitchen towels

Felt-tipped pen

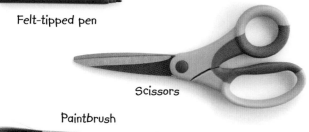

Scissors

Paintbrush

1 With the felt-tipped pen, trace around the end of your phone, halfway along the cardboard tube. Cut along one long side and the two short sides of the rectangle to make a flap. Open up the flap to make a slot.

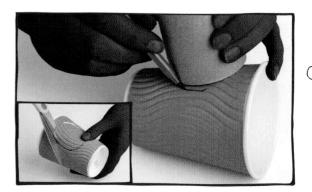

2 Place the end of the tube against the side of one of the paper cups, close to the lip. Hold the tube steady and draw around it with your pen. Cut out the circle you have drawn. Repeat with the other cup.

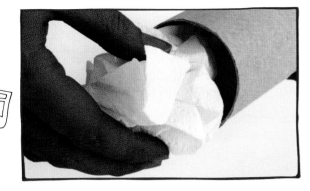

3 Now, tear off two sheets of the paper towel and loosely scrunch them up. Push one crumpled towel into each end of the tube. The paper absorbs some of the high-pitched sounds coming from the tube, so music sounds less tinny.

4 Push one end of the tube a little way into the hole you cut in one of the cups. You may need to use a small amount of force to secure it on. Then fit the other end of the tube into the second cup. You've nearly finished your speakers!

5 The only thing left to do is to paint your speakers in any colours you fancy. When the paint is dry, pop a phone into the slot, with its loudspeakers inside the tube. Then, sit back and enjoy the music!

HOW IT WORKS

Sounds from the mobile phone come out of tiny loudspeakers that vibrate and disturb the air, sending sound waves spreading in all directions. When you put your phone inside your speakers, the sound waves bounce off the insides of the tube and the cups. So nearly all the sound is sent forwards, towards your ears. The crumpled paper stops some of the higher-pitched sounds getting through, but not the lower-pitched ones. This creates a clearer and warmer sound.

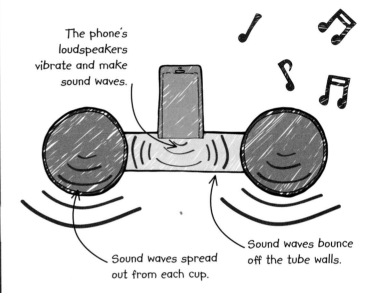

The phone's loudspeakers vibrate and make sound waves.

Sound waves spread out from each cup.

Sound waves bounce off the tube walls.

REAL WORLD SCIENCE
CONCERT LOUDSPEAKERS

At a concert, powerful speakers sit on either side of the stage. Inside each speaker is a cone of paper that vibrates, driven by electrical signals from the equipment – such as an electric guitar – on stage. This produces sound waves that spread out in all directions. Some waves bounce off the back of the speakers and then forwards to the audience.

RUBBER BAND PLANETS

We live on a planet, Earth, that orbits the star we call the Sun. Seven other planets – some bigger and some smaller than Earth – also travel around the Sun. The four planets closest to the Sun, including Earth, are all rocky. The other four, much further away, are made mostly of gas. All these planets, the Sun, and lots of smaller objects, such as moons, are together called the Solar System. You can make beautiful models of all eight planets, showing their colours and relative sizes, using just rubber bands and paper.

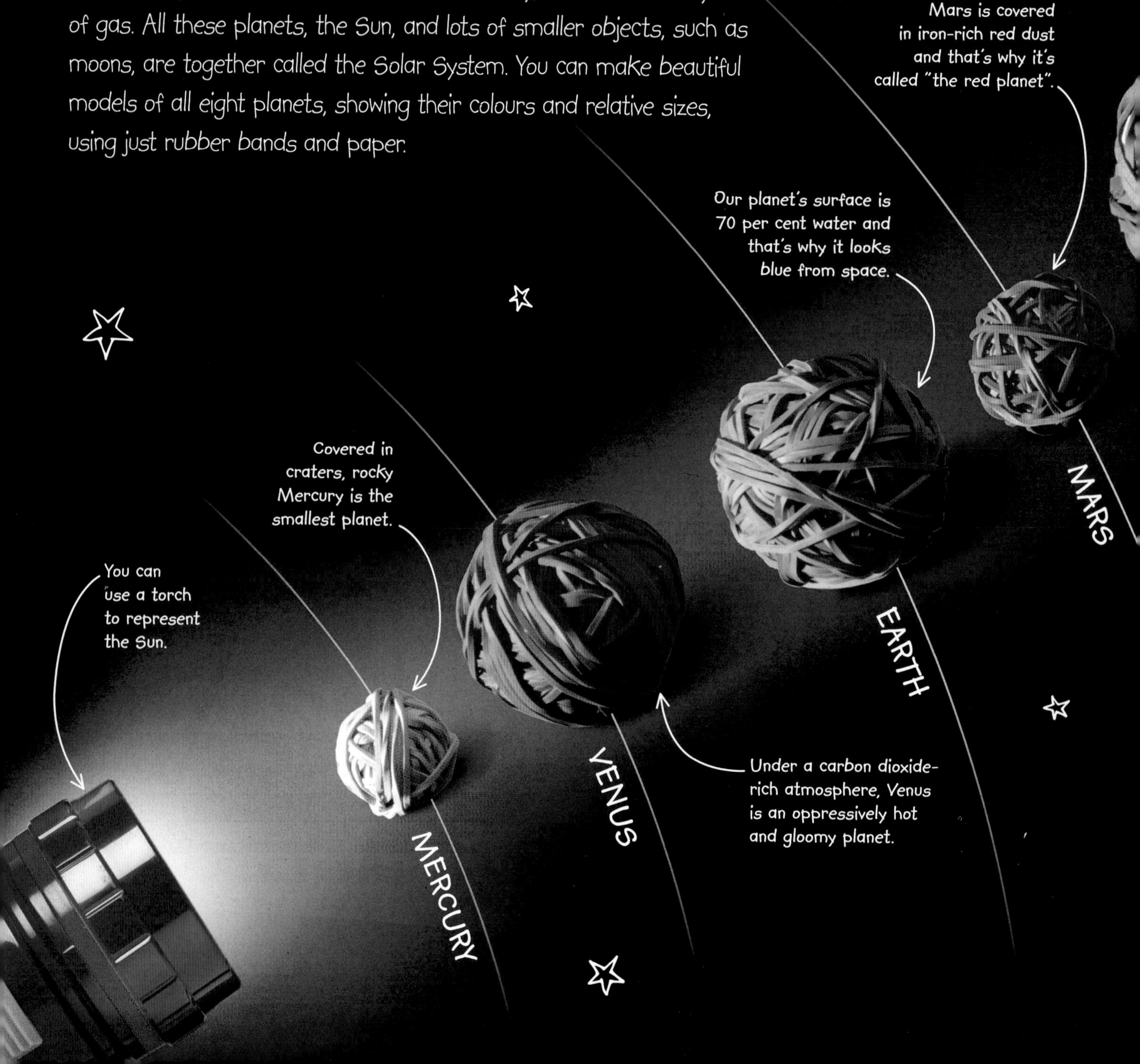

Mars is covered in iron-rich red dust and that's why it's called "the red planet".

Our planet's surface is 70 per cent water and that's why it looks blue from space.

Covered in craters, rocky Mercury is the smallest planet.

You can use a torch to represent the Sun.

Under a carbon dioxide-rich atmosphere, Venus is an oppressively hot and gloomy planet.

MARS

EARTH

VENUS

MERCURY

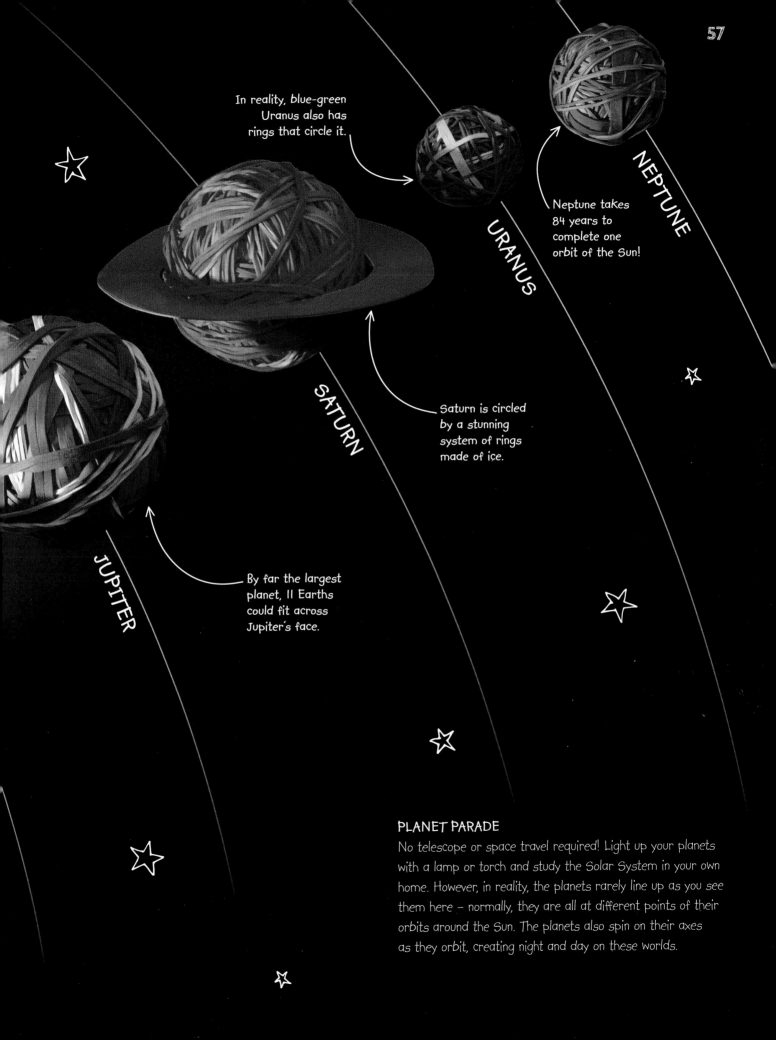

In reality, blue-green Uranus also has rings that circle it.

NEPTUNE

Neptune takes 84 years to complete one orbit of the Sun!

URANUS

SATURN

Saturn is circled by a stunning system of rings made of ice.

JUPITER

By far the largest planet, 11 Earths could fit across Jupiter's face.

PLANET PARADE

No telescope or space travel required! Light up your planets with a lamp or torch and study the Solar System in your own home. However, in reality, the planets rarely line up as you see them here – normally, they are all at different points of their orbits around the Sun. The planets also spin on their axes as they orbit, creating night and day on these worlds.

HOW TO MAKE
RUBBER BAND PLANETS

For your model of the Solar System, you'll need a lot of rubber bands in various colours, but you can buy big bagfuls quite cheaply. You make the planets in order of their distance from the Sun, which will help you to remember their names and where they are in space. The models are not truly to scale, but they do give you a good idea of the sizes of the real planets compared to each other.

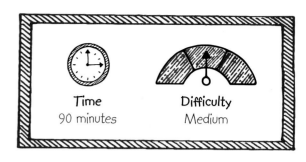

Time
90 minutes

Difficulty
Medium

WHAT YOU NEED

Yellow rubber bands

Green rubber bands

Red rubber bands

White rubber bands

Blue rubber bands

Torch

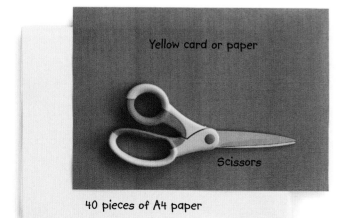

Yellow card or paper

Scissors

40 pieces of A4 paper

Make the paper ball as round as you can and scrunch it tightly.

1 The centre of each planet is a tight ball of scrunched up paper. For the smaller planets, you'll use one piece of paper, or part of one piece. For the bigger planets, you'll scrunch up one piece of paper, then wrap more pieces around it.

2 For Mercury, make the paper ball with just one-quarter of a sheet of paper. Stretch white rubber bands firmly round the ball. Go on adding bands at different angles until you've hidden the paper.

Make sure you put rubber bands at different angles to cover the paper ball completely.

All the planets **revolve** around the Sun in the **same** direction.

Earth is the only known planet to have living things.

3 Make Venus with one piece of paper and yellow and red rubber bands. Venus is reddish-brown, with a rocky surface hidden underneath layers of yellowish-white clouds made of toxic gases.

4 Here comes our own planet, Earth. It is about the same size as Venus, so again needs only one piece of paper. Use lots of blue rubber bands to represent oceans, and some green ones for land.

You could use brown rubber bands, too, if you have some.

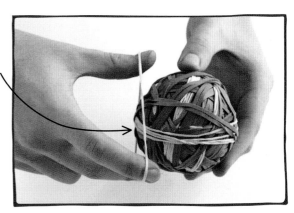

5 Now we've reached Mars, which is about half the size of Earth. Make a paper ball from half a piece of paper and use red bands. Mars is known as "the Red Planet" due to the red dust that covers it.

6 Next is the largest planet in the Solar System, Jupiter. Make the ball with six pieces of paper. Use red, yellow, and white bands to imitate the colourful stripes of Jupiter's dense atmosphere.

7 You can make yellow-brown Saturn, the second largest planet, using five pieces of paper and yellow rubber bands. Saturn is famous for stunning rings made of ice and rock. Cut a ring out of yellow card or paper to fit around the planet.

8 The rings of Saturn don't actually touch the planet, but you'll need to make your cardboard ring fit snugly, or it might fall off.

In reality, Saturn's rings move at very high speeds!

9 Further still from the Sun is the planet Uranus. It is much bigger than Earth, but not as huge as Jupiter or Saturn. Its thick atmosphere is greenish-blue. Use four pieces of paper and green and white rubber bands.

10 The furthest planet from the Sun is Neptune. It is slightly smaller than Uranus, so make it with three pieces of paper. Neptune's atmosphere – which is mostly methane gas – looks blue, so use blue rubber bands.

11 Now that you have made models of all the planets, it's time to line them all up in order, from Mercury to Neptune. In a dark room, use a torch to represent the Sun.

Light takes more than four hours to reach Neptune from the Sun.

Light from the Sun only lights up half of each planet.

Light from the Sun takes eight minutes to reach Earth.

TAKE IT FURTHER

A great way to display your planets is to make a mobile to hang in your bedroom. You'll need to make a model of the Sun. In real life, the Sun's diameter is more than a hundred times that of Earth: for the mobile make it with fifteen pieces of paper and yellow rubber bands.

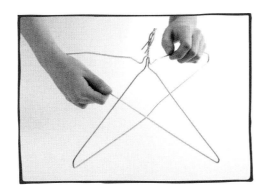

1 To make the mobile, cross over two wire coat hangers and secure them top and bottom with fishing wire or tape. Tie about 30 cm (12 in) of fishing wire around your Sun and planets, so they are secure.

2 Tie the free end of each length of fishing wire around the coat hangers, so the Sun and planets all hang down at different heights. Make sure you put the Sun in the centre. Ask an adult to help you hang your mobile.

HOW IT WORKS

The planets are huge objects hurtling through space. Mercury travels the fastest, with an average speed of more than 170,000 km (105,000 miles) per hour! Despite their high speeds, the planets don't head straight off into space. Instead, they follow orbits, pulled towards the Sun by the force of gravity – the same force that makes you drop back to the ground when you jump in the air. All space bodies, including planets, move in an elliptical orbit. Gravity keeps the Moon and satellites in orbit around Earth, too.

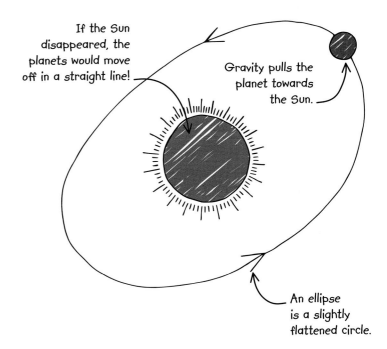

If the Sun disappeared, the planets would move off in a straight line!

Gravity pulls the planet towards the Sun.

An ellipse is a slightly flattened circle.

REAL WORLD SCIENCE
DISTANCE FROM THE SUN

The distances between the Sun and planets are enormous. For scale, if you were to place your model Earth at the correct distance from the torch, they would be 250 metres (820 ft) apart! The distances between planets increases the further out you go.

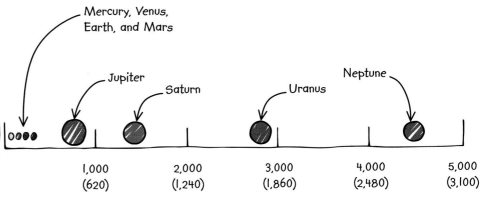

Mercury, Venus, Earth, and Mars

Jupiter

Saturn

Uranus

Neptune

| 1,000 (620) | 2,000 (1,240) | 3,000 (1,860) | 4,000 (2,480) | 5,000 (3,100) |

In million km (miles)

DAZZLING KALEIDOSCOPE

Enjoy a never-ending, dizzying display of colours, shapes, and patterns – no batteries needed! This can be done with a kaleidoscope, a tube that you look down, rather like peering through a telescope. It has mirrors inside and some colourful objects at one end. You can make a kaleidoscope from a cardboard tube, a plastic folder, and a handful of sparkly beads.

Turn the kaleidoscope to see the pattern change – it's never the same twice!

Just add whatever beads you can find: the more colourful they are, the better the effect.

A REFLECTION OF BEAUTY

The beautiful patterns you see when looking down a kaleidoscope are formed when light passes through colourful objects at one end and bounces off reflective surfaces inside. In a shop-bought kaleidoscope, the reflective surfaces are mirrors, but your homemade one using a plastic sheet will produce a terrific display, too.

HOW TO MAKE A
DAZZLING KALEIDOSCOPE

A cardboard tube from a roll of kitchen towel is the perfect size for your kaleidoscope. Inside the tube, you need three reflective surfaces – this can be made from a plastic document folder. However, if you can find it, mirror card also works well. When your kaleidoscope is finished, look through it and point it towards a lamp or out of the window. But remember to never point the tube directly at the Sun, as you could damage your eyes.

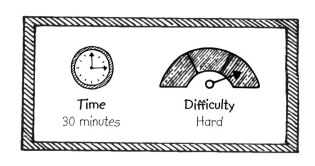

Time
30 minutes

Difficulty
Hard

WHAT YOU NEED

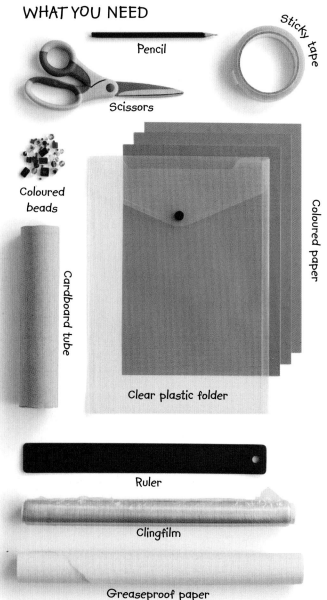

Pencil

Sticky tape

Scissors

Coloured beads

Cardboard tube

Clear plastic folder

Coloured paper

Ruler

Clingfilm

Greaseproof paper

1 Stand the cardboard tube upright on one of the pieces of coloured paper, and draw around the end of the tube. Put the tube to one side, and draw six tabs around the outside edge of the drawn circle. Cut out the circle with the tabs.

Make the hole about 0.5 cm (¼ in) in diameter, and avoid leaving frayed edges.

2 Place the circle over one end of the tube. Stick down the tabs with tape. Make a hole in the centre of the circle with the pencil point. Measure the tube's length and the diameter (width) of the circle.

3 On the plastic folder, draw a rectangle as long as the tube and two and a half times as wide as the tube's diameter. Draw lines to divide the rectangle into three equal parts. Draw a narrow tab on one side.

4 Cut out the rectangle, then score along the three inside lines with the scissors, using the edge of the ruler. Fold along the scored lines to make a triangular prism. Stick down the tab with tape.

5 Insert your prism into the cardboard tube, so that it rests against the paper circle at the end. It should fit snugly, but if not, use small pieces of tape to secure it in place.

6 Place clingfilm loosely over the open end of the tube, and stick it in place with tape. Now put some coloured beads on top of the clingfilm.

7 Cut a circle of greaseproof paper, wider than the tube. Place it over the beads, then cut slits in the edge of the paper and tape it to the tube.

8 Decorate the tube, if you like. Now look through the hole in the paper circle. Point the tube towards a window or light, and turn it around. Enjoy the show!

HOW IT WORKS

At the centre of the pattern you produced by your kaleidoscope is the bead-filled triangle at the end of the cardboard tube. You can see it directly because some of the light that passes through the beads travels straight through the tube. Reflections around the central triangle are made by light that has reflected off one or more of the three shiny surfaces inside the prism. Each surface acts as a mirror, changing the direction the light travels, and so making it appear to have come from behind the mirror.

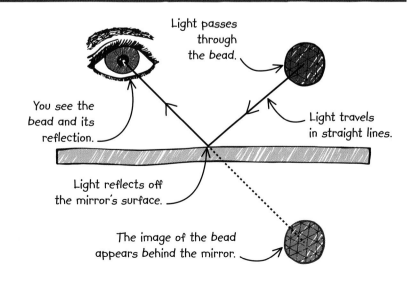

Light passes through the bead.

You see the bead and its reflection.

Light travels in straight lines.

Light reflects off the mirror's surface.

The image of the bead appears behind the mirror.

BALLOON ROCKET CAR

Make a car that speeds along with a few puffs of air. It works in the same way as a jet aeroplane or space rocket, as a stream of fast-moving air escapes from a balloon and shoots out from the back of the car, pushing it forwards. Blow up a balloon and see how far and fast your car can go. Vrroooom!

Think about what shape will make your car faster, so it can slice through the air.

The stretchy balloon squashes the air, maintaining the pressure inside.

Air escaping backwards is what makes the car go forwards.

Wheels grip the road, keeping the car steady.

THE RACE IS ON!

You can make balloon rocket cars with your friends and race against each other. You could even set up a course – a straight one, as there's no steering – and see if you can get your car to cross the finishing line first. How do you think you might be able to make your car go faster and further?

HOW TO MAKE A
BALLOON ROCKET CAR

As the car's body is made of cardboard you'll need to take care when cutting it out, so it doesn't bend or crease. Of course, you can make whatever shape you want – the following instructions will show you just one design. But remember, while you are painting your car put down newspaper or find a place where it doesn't matter if you spill paint!

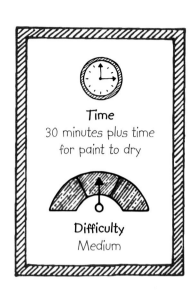

Time
30 minutes plus time for paint to dry

Difficulty
Medium

WHAT YOU NEED

Scissors

Pen

Two wooden skewers

Three bendy straws

Paintbrush

Four bottle tops

Paint (choose your favourite colours)

Balloon

Sticky tape

Double-sided tape

Cardboard

A slightly smaller piece

A larger piece, about 30 x 20 cm (12 x 8 in)

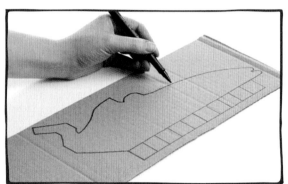

1 On the larger piece of cardboard, draw the shape of your car. Leave space below the car body for a row of rectangles, each about 2 cm (¾ in) wide. For neatness, you can use a ruler. This row will make the tabs for sticking on to the base of the car.

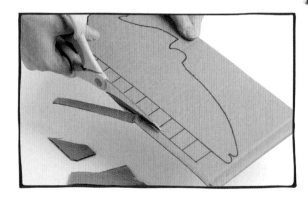

2 Use the scissors to cut around the whole shape. You can cut the lines between the tabs now or wait until step 11, after you paint the car. If you wait, be careful not to paint over the tab lines. Later, they are going to be folded and attached to the base.

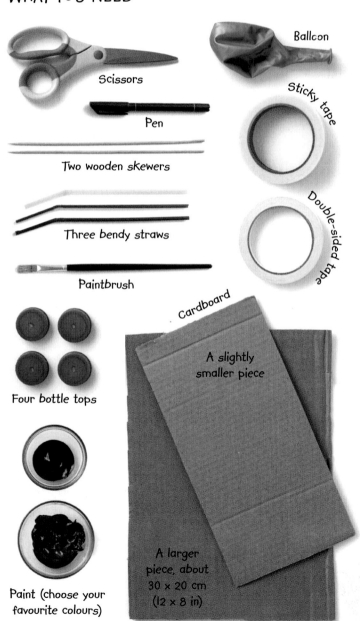

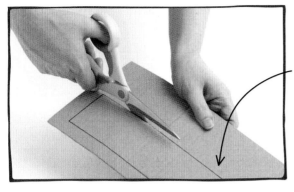

You may want to use a ruler to make sure you keep the lines of your base straight.

3 Now it's time to make the base of the car. Draw and cut out a rectangle, making the longer sides the same length as the total length of the tabs you drew in step 1. The base needs to be only about 3 cm (1¼ in) wide.

4 Your car's wheels are made from the bottle tops. Push the sharp end of a skewer through the centre of each one. A lump of modelling clay will protect your fingers or the work surface. If you have difficulty, ask an adult to help you.

5 Paint the individual pieces before you assemble the car. Choose whatever colours you like, but if you want to create a realistic look, paint both sides of the car body. Put down some newspaper so you don't make a mess!

Only the top side of the car's base needs painting.

You may need to use more than one coat of paint to get the shade you want.

You can paint the wheels, too.

Hold the straw against the car base, so you cut it to the right length.

6 Grab one of your straws and cut it into two pieces that are the same as the width of your car's base. These are to hold the axles in place, and allow the wheels to turn freely.

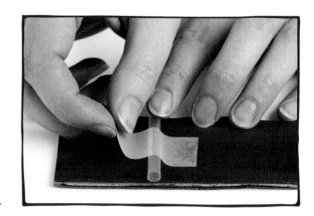

7 Using sticky tape, stick down the straws on the base. Put each straw around 2–3 cm (¾–1¼ in) in from each end, and try to make sure you stick the straws at 90 degrees to the edge.

Mind your fingers! The end of the axle could be splintery.

Watch out, as sometimes the skewer can flip up as it breaks.

8 Cut two pieces of skewer, each about twice the length of the straw and with a point at one end. These are the axles. Of course, be careful when using scissors and don't rush this step.

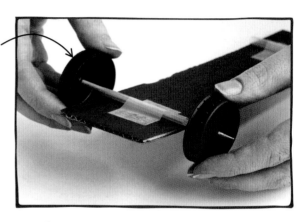

9 Push the point of one axle through one wheel, from the outside. Then push it right through the straw. After that, push the axle through the second wheel from the inside.

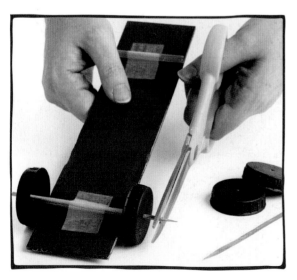

10 For safety, you can cut off the sharp point of the axle. Now repeat step 9 for the other axle and wheel, making sure to take care when pushing the axle through the wheels. If you want, you can also add some sticky tape to the tip of the axles to keep the wheels from falling off.

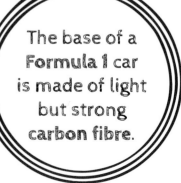

The base of a **Formula 1 car** is made of light but strong **carbon fibre.**

11 Cut the tabs on the car body, if you have not already done so. Fold them back on alternate sides, then add small pieces of double-sided tape to each tab and stick them carefully on to the wheeled base.

You can use glue instead of tape, if you prefer.

Take care when folding the tabs — you don't want to tear them off.

Check that the wheels turn freely to roll the car's base along.

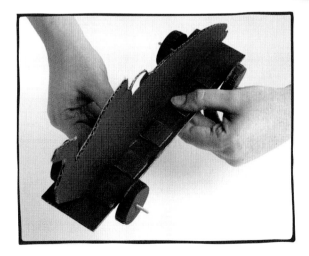

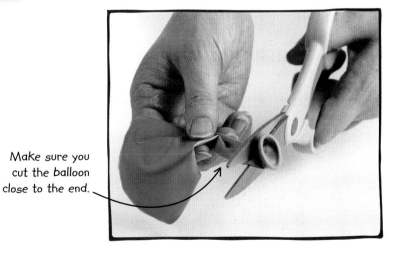

Make sure you cut the balloon close to the end.

12 Check that the tabs are spread out properly and press the body on to the base. Squeeze the tabs firmly, so they stick well. Now you just need a way of making your car go!

13 Cut off the end of the balloon. The power to make your car move comes from air, which is supplied by your breath, then stored and compressed in the balloon.

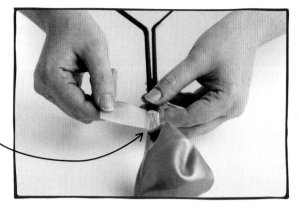

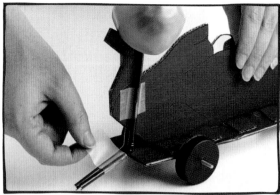

Seal the balloon's neck as well as you can, or the air will leak out.

14 Put the long ends of two bendy straws into the neck of the balloon and wrap some tape around. Make sure you seal the balloon's neck tightly, so that no air can escape.

15 Push the straws down over the back of your car's body and secure them with tape. Bend the short lengths of straw out like exhaust pipes. Use more tape to attach them together.

16 Your car is finished! Hold the neck of the balloon between a thumb and forefinger, and blow into the open ends of the straws. When the balloon is blown up, pinch your finger and thumb together to trap the air inside. Put the car on a flat surface and… let it go!

TAKE IT FURTHER

Try different car bodies, like an empty plastic bottle, shown here. You could have just one straw, to create a better seal so that no air escapes. Now try blowing up the balloon to different sizes. Does the car go further with a larger balloon? Or faster?

Pass the straw through a hole in the side of the bottle.

The bottle's mouth holds the straw horizontal.

Don't forget the wheels!

The size and material of the wheels will impact on the speed of your car. If you have them, try larger wheels made of old DVDs or circles of cardboard. What happens?

Did you choose your lucky number to paint on your car?

HOW IT WORKS

When you *blow up* the *balloon*, the air you breathe out stretches the rubber. The rubber pushes *back* on the air, and the air escapes the only way it can: down the straws and out. When the air meets the *bend* in a straw, it bounces and changes direction, so it can escape horizontally. As the air bounces, it pushes the car forwards. The more air passing out through the straws, the greater the force pushing the car.

High air pressure

The stretched rubber pushes back on the air inside the ballon.

The car moves forwards because the straws expel air.

The escaping air pushes through the straw.

The wheels allow the car to roll.

Air is released from the straws.

REAL WORLD SCIENCE
JET ENGINE

In a jet engine, spinning *turbine* blades draw in air. Heating and compression forms hot gas that escapes through the exhaust nozzle of the aircraft. As this gas shoots backwards, it pushes the aircraft forwards at high speed.

AIR RESISTANCE

Cars are designed to be sleek, creating as little air resistance, or drag, as possible. As a vehicle moves, it pushes air out of the way.

Your car is very thin, so air resistance is not an issue!

Pointed vehicles, such as many sports cars, slice through air – they are streamlined and can move very fast.

Square- or rectangular-shaped vehicles, including buses, experience more drag, which slows them down much more.

STURDY BRIDGE

A single lollipop stick is not very strong, but if you join lots of lollipop sticks together into a rigid structure, they can support surprisingly heavy weights. Test this theory by making your very own bridge using lollipop sticks, glue, and tape. The secret to its strength is all in the triangular design. Once you've made this, you might want to try making longer bridges. If you do, don't forget that triangles are the key to strength.

Connected triangles give this bridge its great strength.

STRONG TRIANGLES

A triangle is a rigid shape. Connecting several triangles together makes them act as one large and rigid object. When a collection of pieces joined together work in this way to act as one, it is called a truss. You will find trusses in almost every structures in the world – and they nearly all have lots of triangles, too.

If you test your bridge's strength with bricks or heavy stones, be careful that they don't drop on your feet!

Paint your mighty bridge in your favourite colour.

HOW TO MAKE A
STURDY BRIDGE

Take your time making this bridge: the more accurately you put the pieces together, and the more time you allow the glue to set, the stronger the finished result will be. Put down some newspaper first, as the glue can get messy. Also, make sure you have enough space to put completed sections of the bridge to one side while you make the other sections.

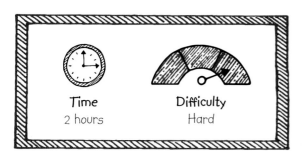

Time
2 hours

Difficulty
Hard

WHAT YOU NEED

PVA glue

Brick

70 lollipop sticks

Masking tape

Press the sticks together, and leave them for a minute for the glue to dry.

1 Start by making one side of the bridge. First glue the ends of three lollipop sticks together to make an equilateral triangle – so all three sides are the same length, and all three angles are equal.

You should end up with a triangle on the end of a line of sticks.

2 Dab glue onto the end of another stick, then press one corner of the triangle on top. Add two more sticks in a line, each under the one before it.

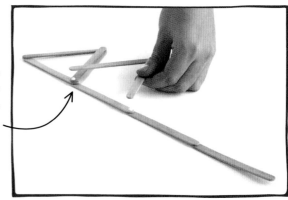

Glue together the ends of the sticks to form another triangle.

3 Glue two more sticks into an equilateral triangle on the next stick in the line. Repeat twice more to give you four triangles in a line.

4 To finish the first side of the bridge, glue three lollipop sticks across the tops of the four triangles, from the top corner of one to the top corner of the next.

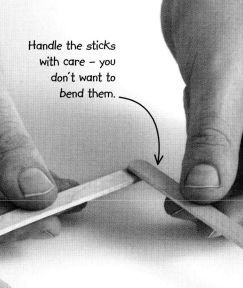

Handle the sticks with care – you don't want to bend them.

It is important to line up the sticks before you glue them together.

You only need a small dab of glue.

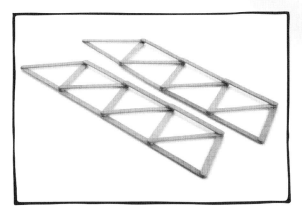

5 Repeat steps 1 to 4 to make the two sides of your bridge. Then leave them somewhere safe while the glue sets.

6 To make the bottom of the bridge, glue the ends of four lollipop sticks together, forming a square. Leave them for a minute so the glue can set.

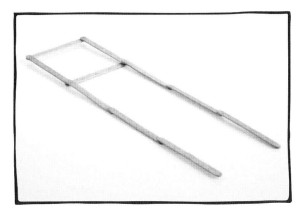

7 Glue three sticks in a line, and stick it to one corner of the square. Glue another line of three sticks to the other corner. Keep the lines parallel.

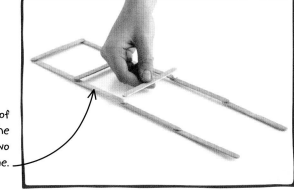

Glue the ends of the stick onto the ends of the two sticks in the line.

8 Make another square by gluing the ends of a stick to the joins of matching sticks in each line. Repeat with two more sticks, making four squares.

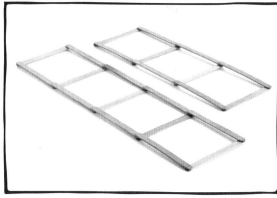

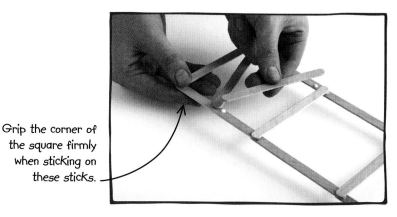

Grip the corner of
the square firmly
when sticking on
these sticks.

9 The top section of your bridge is made in
the same way, but has only three squares.
So repeat steps 6, 7, and 8 with fewer sticks. Now
it's time to strengthen the squares – with triangles!

10 Glue a stick from the corner of a square to
the middle of the stick on the opposite line.
Glue another stick to the opposite corner of the
square to make a triangle. Repeat in each square.

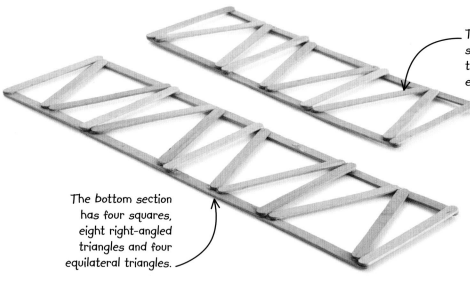

The top section has three
squares, six right-angled
triangles, and three
equilateral triangles.

The bottom section
has four squares,
eight right-angled
triangles and four
equilateral triangles.

11 Once you have strengthened both
the top and bottom sections of
the bridge with triangles, leave them
somewhere safe so that the glue can
begin to set. When the glue has started
to harden, it will be time to put together
all the sections of your bridge.

This is a bit
fiddly, and an
extra pair of
hands from
a friend or an
adult will help.

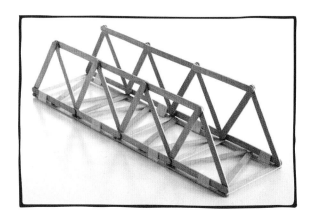

12 Hold the long edge of one side piece at a right
angle to the bottom piece. Tightly wrap masking
tape around the sticks to secure the pieces together.

13 Stick the second side piece to the other side
of the bottom section. The two sides should
be vertical, at right angles to the bottom piece.

14 Attach the top section of your bridge to the side pieces, in the same way as you joined the side pieces to the bottom section. Make sure you wrap the masking tape tightly around the sticks.

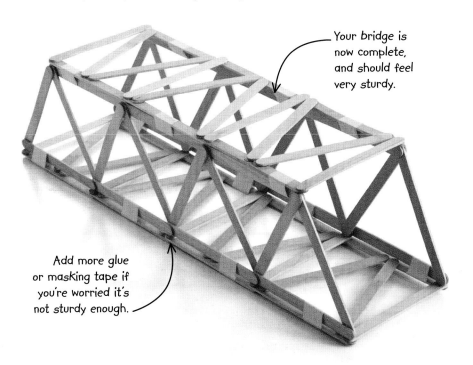

Your bridge is now complete, and should feel very sturdy.

Add more glue or masking tape if you're worried it's not sturdy enough.

15 Choose a safe place to test the strength of your bridge – outside is best. Pick up your brick (or have an adult help you) and place it gently on top of the bridge. What happens? If you have allowed the glue plenty of time to harden, and stuck on enough tape, then hopefully your bridge can carry the weight of one brick. If you have more bricks, add them on very slowly and one at a time.

HOW IT WORKS

When you place a brick on top of your bridge, it pushes down and squashes the sticks in the sides of the bridge. Any solid object that is squashed is said to be "in compression". However, those sticks would move apart if they were not held firmly by the sticks along the bottom of each side. Those sticks are stretched, or "in tension", and support the sticks that are squashed.

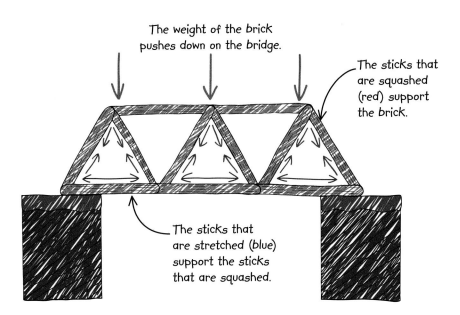

The weight of the brick pushes down on the bridge.

The sticks that are squashed (red) support the brick.

The sticks that are stretched (blue) support the sticks that are squashed.

REAL WORLD SCIENCE
CITY SHAPES

There are lots of triangles in the Sydney Harbour Bridge in Australia, and most bridges. Some materials are better for building with than others, depending on how strong they are when they're in tension and in compression. Using this knowledge, architects and engineers work out what forces a structure can withstand before building begins.

DANCING SNAKE

How would you like to have a new career as a snake charmer and get a writhing serpent to jump up and down and dance as if by magic? You'll have to make use of an invisible force called static electricity. You can create this force with nothing more complicated than tissue paper and a balloon. And, as you'll see, static electricity can do other strange things besides taming paper snakes. It can even bend a stream of water!

Your dancing snake responds to a very safe type of electricity.

It could almost be alive! The balloon gives the snake's head a charge of static electricity and makes it rear up.

HEADS UP

When you put your tissue snake on a table or in the bottom of a basket, its head will normally lie flat. Even light material like this is pulled down by the force of gravity. To lift it up, there must be another force acting on it – one that pulls the snake's head upwards, against gravity. That is the force of attraction between electric charges.

For a real snake-charmer effect, you can put your snake in a basket.

HOW TO MAKE A
DANCING
SNAKE

You need a steady hand to draw and cut out your snake, but otherwise this experiment is as easy as blowing up a balloon! Once you've discovered what static electricity can do to a tissue snake, you can try other things, too. The tiny electric charge involved in the experiment is completely safe. However, you should never investigate the electricity in power cables and appliances; it can *be* very dangerous indeed!

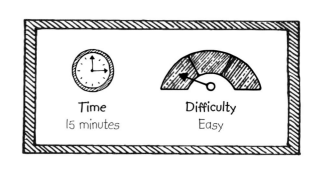

Time
15 minutes

Difficulty
Easy

WHAT YOU NEED

Sticky tape

Balloon

Pens

Scissors

Large plate or bowl

Tissue paper

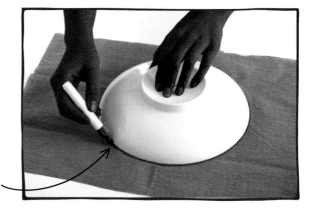

Don't press too hard with the pen, otherwise you might tear the paper.

1 Unfold the tissue paper, so that it is just one sheet thick. For best results, use the thinnest tissue paper you can find. Lay the paper out flat on a table and put the plate upside down on top. Draw around the plate with a pen.

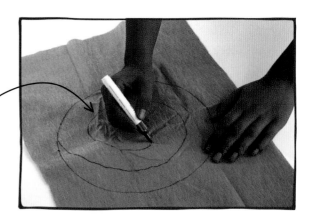

Make the snake's body the same width all the way round.

2 Now draw a spiral on the paper, to create an outline of a coiled-up snake. The centre of the spiral will be the head of the snake, while the tail will be the pointed part around the outside.

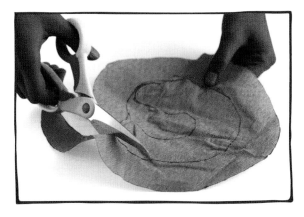

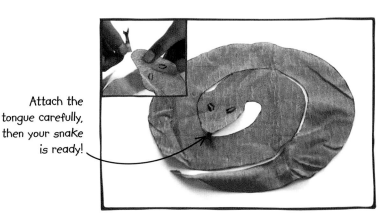

Attach the tongue carefully, then your snake is ready!

3 Cut carefully around the circle you drew and continue along the line of the spiral. As you go round, your snake will be revealed! Tissue paper crumples up very easily, so try not to grip it too hard with your fingers.

4 You can decorate the snake, if you like. Perhaps you could draw on some eyes, or make a small tongue by colouring in some leftover tissue paper with a red pen, then sticking it on. Tape the snake's tail to the table.

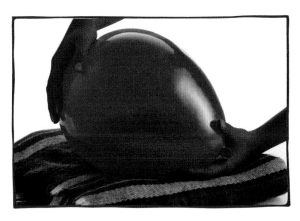

The balloon is now electrically charged.

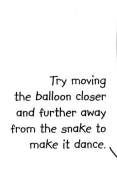

Try moving the balloon closer and further away from the snake to make it dance.

5 Now it's time to generate static electricity. Blow up the balloon and tie it off. Then rub it quite hard against something woollen, such as a jumper, for about a minute. If you don't have anything woollen, you can rub the balloon on your hair.

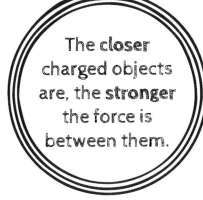

The **closer** charged objects are, the **stronger** the force is between them.

6 Hold the charged balloon a few centimetres above the snake and then slowly bring it closer. When the balloon is about 2 cm (¾ in) above the snake's head, the snake will be attracted to the balloon, and will rise up towards it.

TAKE IT FURTHER

You can explore the forces of static electricity in many ways – here are just a few fun ways, using objects you can find around the home. Charge the *balloons* by rubbing on hair or wool, as before.

BENDING WATER

The invisible forces of static electricity can do surprising things that seem like magic! See for yourself how static electricity can bend water before your very eyes.

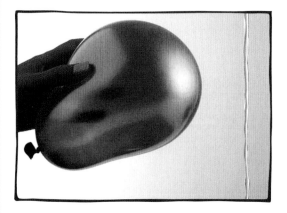

1 Turn on a tap to produce a slow but steady stream of water. Bring an uncharged balloon close to the running water. What happens? Nothing!

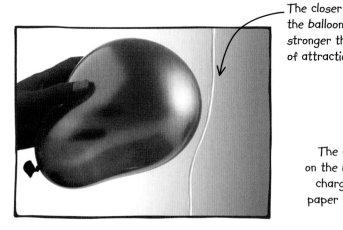

The closer the balloon, the stronger the force of attraction.

2 Now charge up the *balloon* and bring it close to the stream of water. This time the water bends, attracted by the forces of static electricity.

JUMPING PAPER PEOPLE

Make the people dance! You can use a charged *balloon* to attract small pieces of paper on a table. See how close you have to hold the balloon before the paper jumps up and down.

Gravity pulls the paper pieces down towards the surface.

1 Cut out lots of small pieces of paper. The round "confetti" made by a hole punch works well, or you could make fun shapes like these. Lay them on a table.

The charge on the balloon charges the paper pieces.

2 Bring a charged *balloon* close to the paper pieces. The pieces will jump up and stick to the balloon. Some will even fall off and jump up again.

PUSHING BALLOONS

Hang two uncharged *balloons together* and nothing much happens. Yet, when the *balloons are charged* with *static electricity*, things start to get a little more interesting.

1 Tie string to each of two balloons. Do not charge them yet, but hold both strings between a finger and thumb and let the balloons hang down.

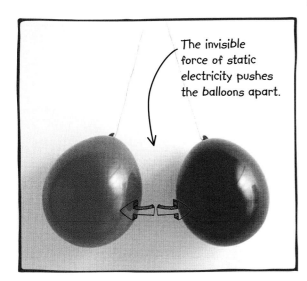

The invisible force of static electricity pushes the balloons apart.

2 Charge both balloons evenly, all over their surfaces. When you dangle them down now, they stay apart, repelled (pushed) by an invisible force.

HOW IT WORKS

Electric charge is carried by tiny particles called protons, which carry a positive (+) charge, and electrons, which carry a negative (-) charge. Charges exert forces on each other: charges of the same type push apart, or repel, while opposite charges pull together, or attract. Normally, there are equal numbers of positive and negative charges everywhere. However, when you rub the balloon on wool or your hair it picks up extra electrons, giving the balloon an overall negative charge. This pushes the electrons away in the paper, making the paper's edge positively charged. That is why the paper snake is attracted to the balloon.

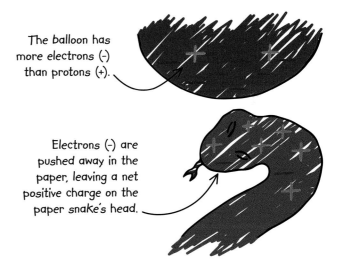

The balloon has more electrons (-) than protons (+).

Electrons (-) are pushed away in the paper, leaving a net positive charge on the paper snake's head.

REAL WORLD SCIENCE
LIGHTNING STORM

Inside a thundercloud, swirling winds make ice crystals in the cloud rub together, which charges them. The base of ths cloud becomes negatively charged, which is attracted to a positively charged ground. This can produce lightning, which takes the shortest route to the ground, often striking trees.

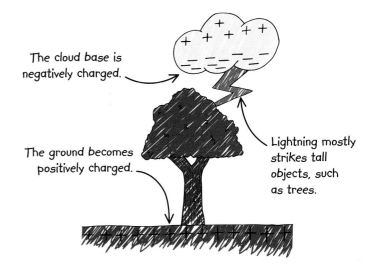

The cloud base is negatively charged.

The ground becomes positively charged.

Lightning mostly strikes tall objects, such as trees.

BREATHING MACHINE

Before you start this experiment, take a deep breath. Have you ever stopped to wonder how your body manages to take in big gulps of life-giving air into your lungs and then breathe it out again? It's all due to air pressure, and a very special muscle in your abdomen called the diaphragm. With a bottle, some balloons, and several straws – plus a few other bits and bobs you'll find around your home – you can easily make a model that shows how we breathe.

The two straws represent tubes called bronchi, through which air passes into the balloon lungs.

The two red balloons represent your lungs.

The plastic bottle represents your chest and abdomen.

A blue balloon attached to the bottom of the bottle represents a muscle called the diaphragm.

AIR IN, AIR OUT

You need to breathe in order to take in oxygen from the air. Inside your lungs, oxygen passes through the walls of tiny blood vessels and into your blood. The blood carries the oxygen all around your body, and every one of your cells uses some of it, producing carbon dioxide as a waste product. Your blood carries the carbon dioxide to your lungs, and it moves into the air inside your lungs, ready to be breathed out when you exhale.

HOW TO MAKE A
BREATHING MACHINE

This is a great way to learn how some vital parts of your body work. You can construct your model lungs using materials you can find around the home. The experiment isn't really that difficult, but you need to follow the instructions very carefully if you want your breathing machine to work well – making joins airtight is particularly important. Use glue as well as tape or adhesive putty, if you find this makes things easier.

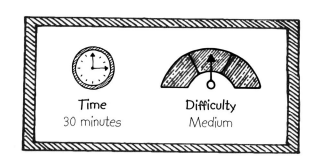

Time
30 minutes

Difficulty
Medium

WHAT YOU NEED

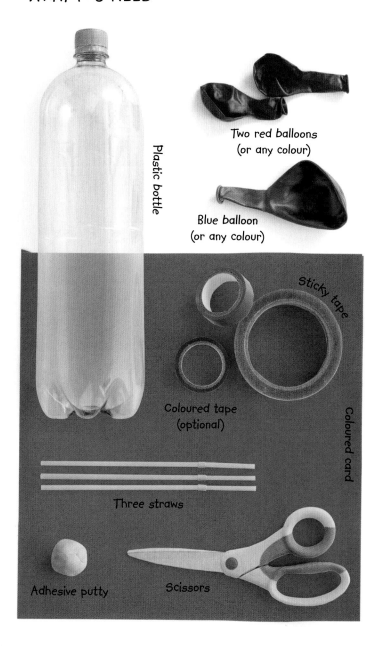

Plastic bottle

Two red balloons
(or any colour)

Blue balloon
(or any colour)

Sticky tape

Coloured tape
(optional)

Coloured card

Three straws

Adhesive putty

Scissors

1 Cut off the base of the bottle. Keep the cut nice and straight, as it will help you to make an airtight seal on the bottom of the bottle later on. Ask for help if you're not sure you can do this. Save the bottle cap – you're going to need it later.

2 Cut all three straws to just over 10 cm (4 in). One of the straws will represent the trachea, the name of the breathing tube that joins the back of your throat to the top of your lungs.

3 Now cut off the ends of both red balloons. In your model, the *balloons* will represent the lungs. They will take in air and let it out again, inflating and deflating inside the bottle as if breathing in and breathing out.

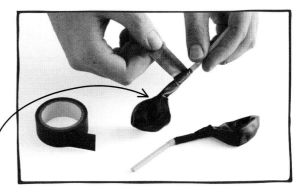

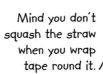

Mind you don't squash the straw when you wrap tape round it.

4 Push the end of one straw about 2 cm (¾ in) inside a balloon. Wrap tape firmly around the *balloon*, making an airtight join. Now repeat with the other balloon and another straw. These straws represent branching air tubes called *bronchi*.

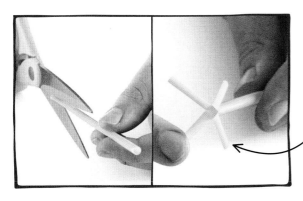

5 Cut a slit 2 cm (¾ in) up the middle of one end of the third straw – the *trachea* – so that it opens up into two equal parts. Do the same at the other end, then turn the straw 90 degrees and cut it again, so this end opens into four equal parts.

This end of the straw represents the air passage at the back of your throat.

Like real lungs, the balloons will inflate when they fill with air.

Make sure the joins are airtight.

A person breathes in and out about **seven million times** every year.

6 Push the two straws (the *bronchi*) with the two *balloons* attached (the lungs) over the ends of each half of the two-way split straw (the *trachea*). Finally, secure them with sticky tape.

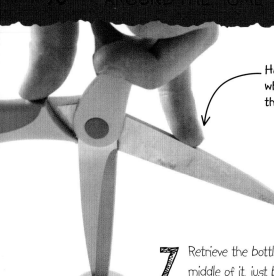

Hold the scissors firmly when pushing and turning the scissors into the cap.

When you have positioned the straw, screw the cap onto the bottle.

7 Retrieve the bottle cap and cut a hole in the middle of it, just big enough for a straw to fit. Keep your fingers clear of the scissors' point and don't jab the table by mistake! To avoid mishaps, you can push the cap into a lump of adhesive putty.

8 Now pick up the end of the "trachea straw" that is split into four. Hold the four flaps together and push them right through the hole in the bottle cap. Once the flaps are through the hole, fold them down to lie against the top of the cap.

Keep the tape tightly stretched as you wind it around the cap.

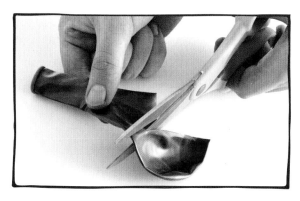

9 Check that the straw fits snugly in the hole. Then, using tape, make a tight seal around the bottle cap to stop air leaking into the bottle through tiny gaps.

10 Cut the third balloon just beyond the end of the neck. This represents a sheet of muscle called the diaphragm. Hint: if you inflate it before you do the cut, it will be easier to stretch in step 11.

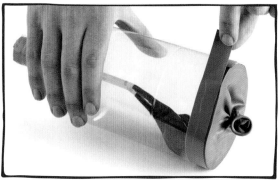

Push the third balloon firmly so that all of the air escapes.

11 Tie off the end of the balloon, as you would have if you had just blown it up. Stretch it over the end of the bottle and secure it with tape. Make sure the join is completely airtight.

12 Your working model is now complete! To make it breathe in, pull the end of the balloon; to breathe out, push it up again. Watch the balloon lungs inflate and deflate.

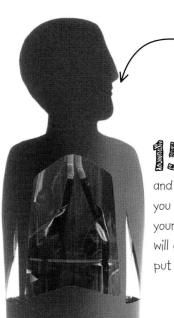

13 Draw and cut out a net. You don't have to be an artist: the important thing is to cut a large hole in the middle figure. At the base of the net, cut a tab at one end and a slit at the other.

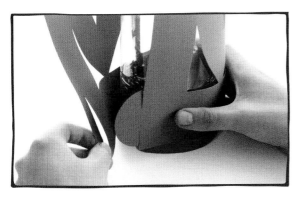

14 Wrap the net around your model, and tuck the tab into the slit. Add sticky tape to make the tab more secure. Your "breathing" lungs should appear through the middle hole.

This head and body cut out puts the lungs in context.

15 The paper wraparound head and body will really help you explain to others what your model is showing – it will also look great if you put your model on display.

HOW IT WORKS

Breathing is all about pressure. When you pull down on the balloon, you increase the volume inside the bottle, reducing the air pressure inside. This makes the air from outside the bottle rush through the straw and inflate both balloons. When you push the balloon up, you reduce the volume and increase the pressure inside the bottle, so the air rushes out again.

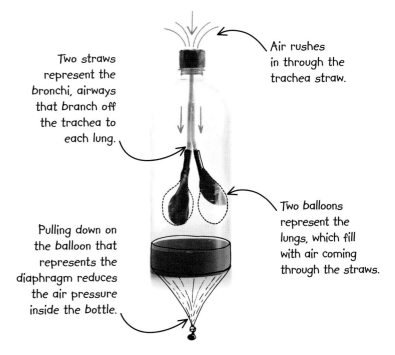

Two straws represent the bronchi, airways that branch off the trachea to each lung.

Air rushes in through the trachea straw.

Two balloons represent the lungs, which fill with air coming through the straws.

Pulling down on the balloon that represents the diaphragm reduces the air pressure inside the bottle.

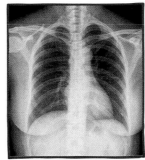

REAL WORLD SCIENCE
CHEST CAVITY

In this X-ray, you can see the lungs (black) either side of the spine (white), protected by the ribs (also white). The diaphragm is the large grey structure at the bottom.

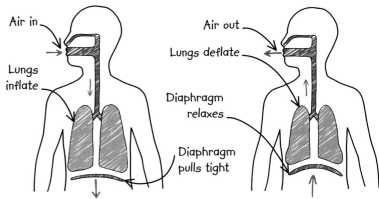

Air in

Lungs inflate

As you breathe in, or inhale, your lungs inflate and your diaphragm flattens and pushes downwards.

Air out

Lungs deflate

Diaphragm relaxes

Diaphragm pulls tight

As you breathe out, or exhale, your lungs deflate and your diaphragm is pushed upwards.

WATER WORLD

Turn on a tap in the kitchen or bathroom and you have an instant supply of one of the most important substances in the Universe: water. In this chapter, you'll be exploring some of the remarkable properties of water, which we know can be a liquid, a solid, and a gas. These experiments will help you to understand about the forces within water and how it behaves with other substances. Water is awash with science – so dive in!

DENSITY TOWER

Make an eye-catching tower in a glass by layering coloured liquids one above another. It looks like a magic trick, but it works because liquids of different densities, such as oil and water, don't mix together. In this experiment, the most dense liquids form the bottom of the tower and the least dense float on top. You'll find most of the things you need for your tower in the kitchen cupboard. So, let's get building!

Oil floats at the top because it is the least dense of all the liquids used in the tower.

A ping pong ball has a low density because it is filled with air. Drop it in the tower and see what happens.

SINK OR FLOAT?

The density of a substance is related to its mass (how much matter there is) and its volume (how much space it takes up). When you've made the tower, try another experiment to test the density of the liquids. Choose a few small objects, such as the ones pictured here, and drop them into the tower to see whether they sink or float. A liquid can support anything that is less dense than itself.

A small tomato will sink through layers of oil, water, and washing-up liquid but float on top of milk.

HOW TO MAKE A
DENSITY TOWER

You'll need a steady hand to build this tower in neat layers. Most of the liquids are "water-based", meaning they are composed of water but with other substances dissolved in it. The following instructions show you how to make the layers using a turkey baster, but it's fine just to dribble the liquids over the back of a spoon. After adding each liquid, remember to wash the baster or spoon before going on to the next layer. Don't stir the tower or these liquids will get mixed up.

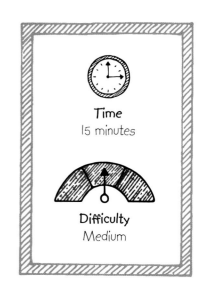

Time
15 minutes

Difficulty
Medium

WHAT YOU NEED

Water with food colouring

Vegetable oil

Milk

Washing-up liquid

Runny honey

Tall, straight-sided glass

Ping pong ball

Cherry tomato

Bolt

Turkey baster

1 The first layer of your tower is honey. This is the densest of the liquids. Carefully pour it in until it reaches about 2 cm (¾ in) up the glass. Honey is water with many other substances, mostly sugars, dissolved in it.

2 Next, put in the milk. Draw it up with the turkey baster and gently dribble it against the side of the glass. It will settle on top of the honey. Milk is water with proteins, sugars, and tiny globules of oil.

For a **stunning density tower**, add each liquid **slowly** and **carefully.**

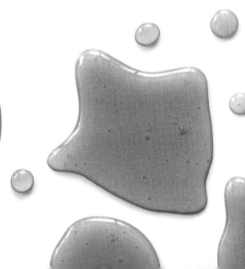

3 Make this layer just as you did in step 2. Draw up the washing-up liquid with the baster and trickle it in slowly against the side of the glass. Washing-up liquid is water with large detergent molecules dissolved in it.

4 You're now ready to add the fourth layer, which is water. You can make this any colour you like by adding a few drops of food colouring. Remember to trickle the liquid slowly! Water molecules are very small and tightly packed.

5 Finally, add vegetable oil, although olive oil also works. Interestingly, if you had put the oil in first instead of last, it would still have risen to the top because it's the least dense liquid – but you would spoil your tower!

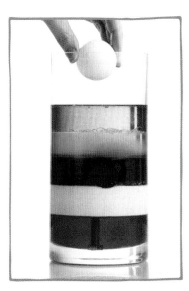

6 Now gently drop in small objects, like a bolt, tomato, and ping pong ball. The bolt sinks to the bottom because it is denser than the honey. The tomato sinks until it meets the milk. What happens to the ping pong ball?

HOW IT WORKS

Although water molecules crowd closely together, each one has low mass, so water's density is fairly low. When substances dissolve in water, their molecules sneak in between the water molecules, increasing the solution's density. Oil molecules are bigger and do not pack together so tightly, which means it has a low density.

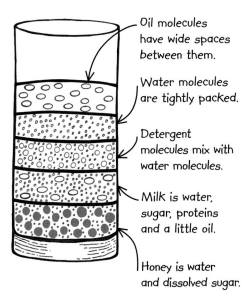

Oil molecules have wide spaces between them.

Water molecules are tightly packed.

Detergent molecules mix with water molecules.

Milk is water, sugar, proteins and a little oil.

Honey is water and dissolved sugar.

REAL WORLD SCIENCE
OIL SPILL

Occasionally, tanker ships carrying oil accidentally spill their contents. This is bad for sea life, and an oil spill is difficult to clean up. What makes the task a bit easier is the fact that oil floats on water. The oil can be scooped up out of the water or sprayed with detergents, which helps to dissolve it.

The stream of water has energy and some is transferred to the waterwheel's blades.

The faster the flow, the faster the waterwheel turns.

Some of the water's energy is lost as it splashes off the waterwheel's blades.

The waterwheel sits in a frame made from a plastic bottle.

FEEL THE ENERGY

A waterwheel is an "energy-transfer device". Like anything that moves, flowing water possesses a form of energy called kinetic energy. Your waterwheel will capture some of that energy and begin turning. A string wrapped around the shaft of your waterwheel can lift a weight. As the weight lifts higher up, it gains potential energy (it has the "potential" to fall down again), also called stored energy.

The string coils around the wooden skewer as the weight is raised.

WATERWHEEL

Question: how can you lift a weight just by turning on a tap or pouring water from a jug? Answer: with a waterwheel, of course. Waterwheels have been used to extract energy from flowing water for many hundreds of years – to grind corn, power machinery, or lift heavy objects. You can make your own waterwheel from a plastic bottle, a straw, and a wooden skewer. It'll create quite a splash!

The waterwheel lifts a weight made of adhesive putty.

HOW TO MAKE A
WATERWHEEL

To make your waterwheel, you have to cut up a plastic bottle: this can be a little bit tricky, so ask an adult if you need help. The other thing to watch out for is using a wooden skewer to make the shaft of the waterwheel. You might want to cut off any sharp points before you begin. And don't forget that water is wet, so when you're ready to test your waterwheel, take it outside or place it in a large sink.

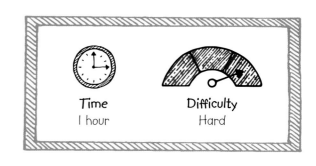

Time
1 hour

Difficulty
Hard

WHAT YOU NEED

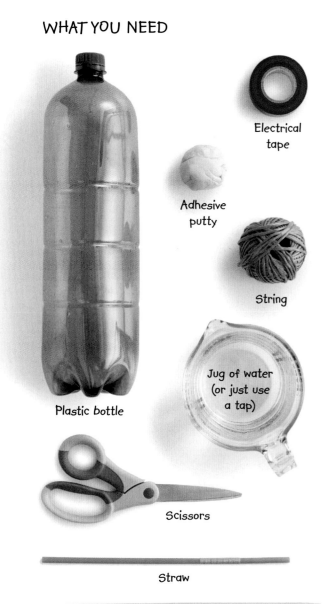

Plastic bottle

Adhesive putty

Electrical tape

String

Jug of water (or just use a tap)

Scissors

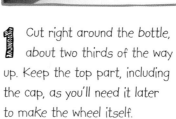

Straw

Wooden skewer

Ask an adult for help if you find this step difficult.

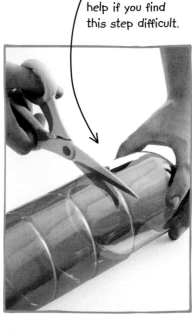

1 Cut right around the bottle, about two thirds of the way up. Keep the top part, including the cap, as you'll need it later to make the wheel itself.

Leave enough of the bottle's sides to make a sturdy frame.

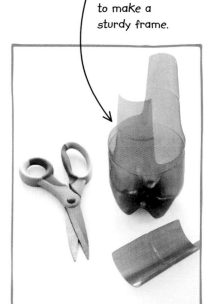

2 Next, cut out two U-shaped pieces from the sides of the bottle, as shown. What you have now is the frame that will support the waterwheel.

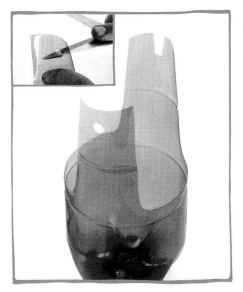

3 With the point of the scissors, carefully make a small hole in one side of the frame. Then cut a notch in the opposite side, level with the hole.

4 Now get the top part of the bottle, and make six evenly spaced cuts that end level with each other at the neck. These flaps will actually be the blades.

5 Fold each of the six blades back on itself and crease the fold. Try to keep all the folds level, cutting a little deeper if you need to.

Don't make the cuts too long, or the blades may tear off.

If you crease the folds well, each blade should have an angle of about 90 degrees.

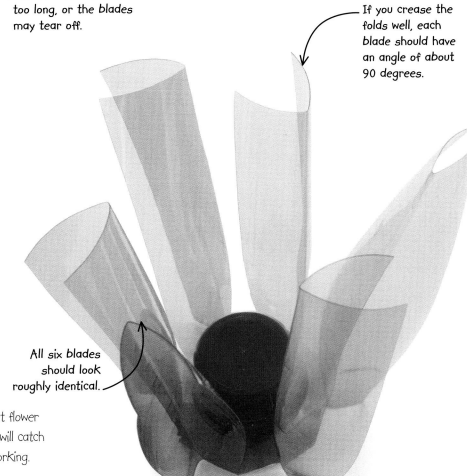

6 Cut halfway along the base of each blade, where it joins the bottle neck. Then fold each blade in half along its length and crease it.

All six blades should look roughly identical.

7 Bend the splayed wheel into a compact flower shape. This makes the surfaces that will catch the falling water once you get your wheel working.

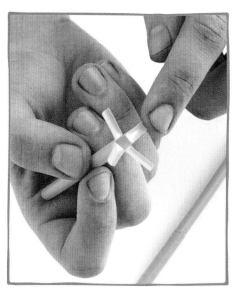

8 The blades of the waterwheel have to fit inside the frame and *be able* to turn around easily. To achieve this, hold the waterwheel next to the frame and trim the blades to the right length.

9 Remove the bottle cap and pierce a hole through it. You have to push hard, *so secure the cap in some adhesive putty – and mind your fingers!* Screw the cap *back* onto the wheel.

10 Cut the straw so you have a straight part, about 5 cm (2 in) long. Carefully snip one end into four sections. Fold the sections down at right angles to the straw.

You can snip the sharp end of the skewer once it's through the bottle cap.

Electrical tape holds the straw firmly on the skewer.

Check that the wheel turns freely.

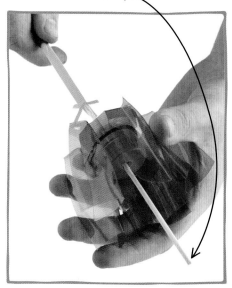

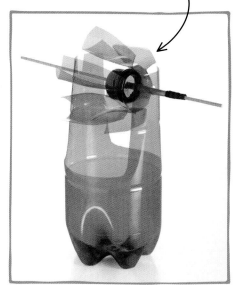

11 Slide the skewer through the straw and tape the straw onto it, about 3 cm (1½ in) from the end. Then push the wooden skewer through the hole in the bottle cap.

12 Pack adhesive putty into the bottle cap to secure the cut sections at the end of the straw. Now try turning the skewer with your fingers. The waterwheel should turn, too!

13 Push one side of the skewer through the hole in the *base* of the bottle, resting the other side in the open notch. The bottle cap should not touch the side of the frame.

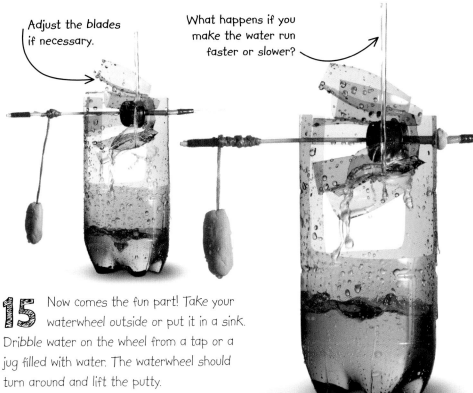

Adjust the blades if necessary.

What happens if you make the water run faster or slower?

14 Tape a piece of string near the end of the skewer without the straw. Then press a lump of adhesive putty around the other end of the string – this will act as a weight.

15 Now comes the fun part! Take your waterwheel outside or put it in a sink. Dribble water on the wheel from a tap or a jug filled with water. The waterwheel should turn around and lift the putty.

HOW IT WORKS

When you pour the water, it exerts a force on the *blades* of the waterwheel, making them turn. The shaft exerts a force on the wooden skewer, turning it. As the skewer turns, it also applies a force on the attached string, which pulls up the adhesive putty weight.

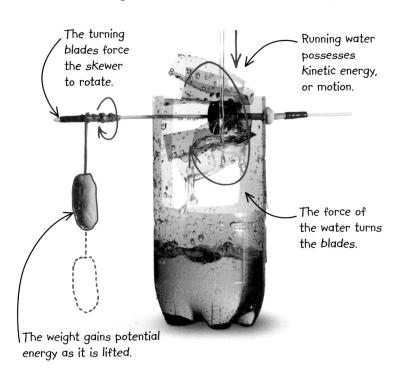

The turning blades force the skewer to rotate.

Running water possesses kinetic energy, or motion.

The force of the water turns the blades.

The weight gains potential energy as it is lifted.

REAL WORLD SCIENCE
HYDROELECTRICITY

Flowing water can be used to generate electricity. In a hydroelectric power station, river water is held back by a dam, so that it builds up huge pressure and lots of potential energy. It flows under pressure through pipes, turning specially designed waterwheels called turbines. These, then, turn electric generators that supply many homes and businesses with electricity. This picture shows the top of the shafts of several turbines that spin horizontally. The generators are inside the round blue part at the top of each turbine.

SOAP-POWERED BOAT

Get ready to set sail on the soapy seven seas! Make a little boat, float it on some water, and then – using nothing but a dab of washing-up liquid – send it whizzing across the surface. The soap doesn't really power the boat but it releases hidden energy in the water. Hoist anchor and have a go!

This cut-out area is where the washing-up liquid goes, acting as a kind of "fuel" for the boat.

Decorate your boat with any type of flag you choose.

DESIGNER FLEET

Get together with your friends to make a whole fleet of boats and have races. You don't have to use the same design every time. Branch out with some experiments of your own and try different shapes and see which boats move fastest.

Invisible forces in the water pull your boat along.

HOW TO MAKE A
SOAP-POWERED BOAT

This boat has to be light to zoom along propelled only by tiny forces in the water. The materials you use weigh almost nothing and are easy to cut into the right shapes. But if you don't want to do the cutting out yourself, ask an adult to help you. The boat shown here has a very simple design, so you can make it very quickly and get sailing straight away. Paint your boat in any colour you like.

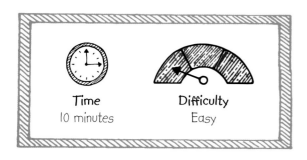

Time	Difficulty
10 minutes	Easy

WHAT YOU NEED

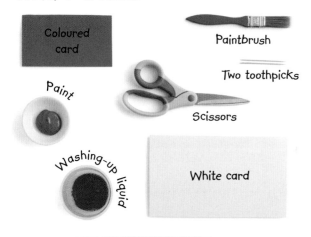

Coloured card

Paintbrush

Paint

Two toothpicks

Scissors

Washing-up liquid

White card

Tray with water inside it

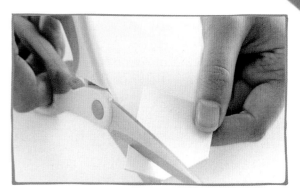

1 Start by making the hull, or base, of the boat. Use your scissors to cut out a small square of white card, with each side of the square measuring about 4 cm (1½ in). Cut a point at one end to make the bow, or front, of the boat.

2 Cut out a 0.5 cm (¼ in) square notch at the back, or stern, of your boat. This is the end where you'll put the washing-up liquid. If you like, you can try out other sizes and shapes for the notch.

3 For the sail, cut out a piece of coloured card and put a toothpick through it. The sail won't move your boat, but it looks good. Then paint your boat with any colours that you like.

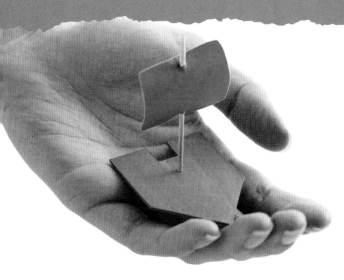

4 When the paint dries completely, it's time to secure the toothpick sail to the boat. Your boat is ready to set sail!

5 Float your boat on the water-filled tray – keep it close to one corner and point it towards the middle. Dip a toothpick in washing-up liquid and touch the water's surface, in the notch at the boat's stern.

6 Watch your boat go! Just keep dipping the toothpick in the washing-up liquid and touching it to the notch. But if the water gets too soapy, you'll need to change it or the experiment won't work.

HOW IT WORKS

This soapy experiment makes use of something called surface tension – because water molecules cling together, they pull each other in all directions. This motion pulls tight the surface of the water, like the skin of a balloon. But when you drop washing-up liquid into the water, the bonds behind the boat weaken, reducing surface tension. As a result, the rest of the water surface pulls away, dragging the boat along with it.

As soon as you apply the washing-up liquid, it quickly spreads in all directions.

The boat pulls away, as the washing-up liquid weakens the bonds between the water molecules.

Surface tension is due to **invisible forces** pulling water molecules together.

REAL WORLD SCIENCE
BLOWING BUBBLES

Have you ever wondered why you can't blow bubbles with just water? It's because the surface tension is so strong you can't make the water stretch into a different shape. Mixing in soap reduces the surface tension enough for you to blow air inside the water without the bubble collapsing immediately.

FABULOUS FILTER

Imagine having to drink from rivers, lakes, or ponds – like lots of people in the world do – instead of turning on a tap or opening a bottle to get pure clean water. You'd have to find a way of removing mud and other unpleasant substances mixed in the water before quenching your thirst. In this experiment, you'll make a simple water-filtering device using a plastic bottle. Watch dirty water becoming cleaner before your very eyes!

DIRTY WATER

Water that comes straight from natural sources often carries impurities that could make you ill if you drank them. You can easily remove leaves, twigs, and dead bugs floating on the surface. Yet, mixed up in dirty water there are millions of smaller particles, some of which carry bacteria and viruses that you simply can't see. How do you get rid of those? The answer is, you have to make a trap to catch them.

Put charcoal into your filter to help clean the water.

Pieces of clean gravel help to trap particles floating about in dirty water.

Dirty water is filtered through several layers of different materials.

The experiment will produce cleaner water – but not good enough for you to drink.

HOW TO MAKE A
FABULOUS FILTER

Making a water filter is just the first part of this experiment. You'll also be making your own dirty water to test it! The materials you need are not hard to get, but you might have to ask an adult to help you look for some of them. Even though the completed filter does a pretty good job, the water that passes through it still won't be safe enough to drink. So just pour it away afterwards.

Time	Difficulty
25 minutes	Medium

WHAT YOU NEED

Charcoal

Spoon

Cotton wool balls

Scissors

Leaves and grass

Sand

Small, clean pebbles

Small gravel

Soil

Medium-sized gravel

Measuring jug

Plastic bottle

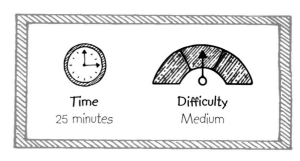

1 First, cut right around the bottle with the scissors, just above halfway up. If you find this tricky, ask an adult to do it for you. The top part is going to be the filter. The bottom part makes a holder for the top and collects the water.

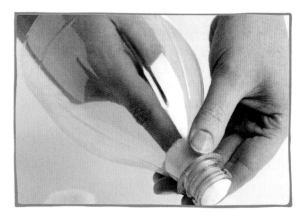

2 If your bottle has a cap, remove it. Tightly pack the cotton wool balls into the mouth of the bottle. These will trap very small pieces of dirt floating in the water.

3 Put the top part of the bottle upside down into the bottom part of the bottle. Add a layer of charcoal, about 1 cm (½ in) deep, on top of the cotton wool. If your charcoal is in big chunks, crush it first to break it into smaller pieces.

4 Add sand about 2 cm (¾ in) deep. Press it hard with your fingertips to push down the sand and the charcoal beneath it. These packed layers will slow down water flow and trap lots of dirt.

5 Next, add a 1 cm (½ in) layer of the small gravel. On top of that, add a 2 cm (¾ in) layer of medium-sized gravel. You must pack these two layers as firmly as you can, just as you did with the sand and the charcoal.

The more layers you add, the cleaner your water will get as it filters down.

6 Finally, add the small pebbles. Make sure you completely cover the top of the gravel. See how the gaps between the particles of each layer have grown bigger and bigger towards the top. Now that your water filter is ready to put to work, you need to make some dirty water!

7 Fill your jug with water and tip in as much of the soil as you like. Stir it all up with a spoon, so that the soil mixes in thoroughly. The smallest pieces of soil will be "suspended" – left floating – in the water, and some parts will dissolve.

These objects from nature won't look pretty for long, as they get mixed up in the dirty water.

Soil particles contain tiny living organisms, such as bacteria.

8 Drop in a few leaves and blades of grass. Your water is now well and truly dirty! It contains particles of many different sizes and various dissolved substances. Any of these things might make you ill if you drank the water.

In a river or pond, leaves and grass would float on top of the water.

Don't forget to wash the jug thoroughly when you've finished your experiment!

9 Slowly pour some dirty water onto the pebbles at the top of your filter. Hold the filter steady to make sure it doesn't topple over. Watch as the water trickles through the layers, and emerges much cleaner at the bottom.

HOW IT WORKS

Water always finds a path through the pieces of stone, gravel, sand, charcoal, and cotton wool. But the gaps, or pores, trap particles that are suspended in the water. As the pores get smaller in each layer, particles are trapped throughout the filter, rather than all in one layer, which would quickly get clogged up. The charcoal removes some of the dissolved substances from the water, purifying the water in a process called adsorption.

Remember! Your filtered water is **not safe to drink**, even if it looks clean.

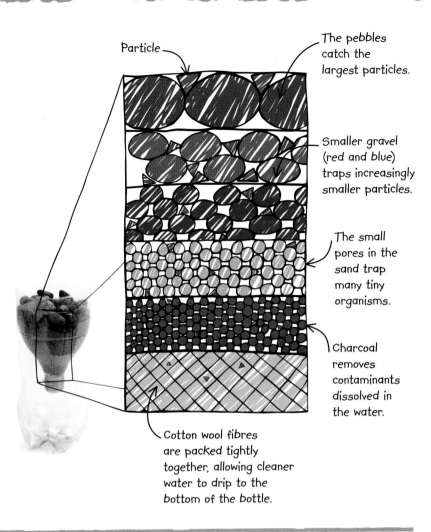

Particle

The pebbles catch the largest particles.

Smaller gravel (red and blue) traps increasingly smaller particles.

The small pores in the sand trap many tiny organisms.

Charcoal removes contaminants dissolved in the water.

Cotton wool fibres are packed tightly together, allowing cleaner water to drip to the bottom of the bottle.

REAL WORLD SCIENCE
LIFE-SAVING STRAW

After a disaster like an earthquake or a flood, it may be impossible to find clean water. The LifeStraw is a filter that allows people to drink directly from any source of water, however dirty. Packed with thin fibres the straw's pores trap tiny organisms that could otherwise cause illness.

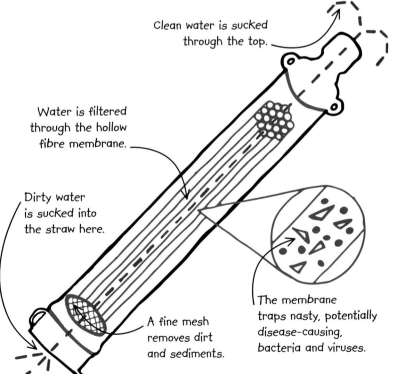

Clean water is sucked through the top.

Water is filtered through the hollow fibre membrane.

Dirty water is sucked into the straw here.

A fine mesh removes dirt and sediments.

The membrane traps nasty, potentially disease-causing, bacteria and viruses.

STUNNING STALACTITE

Inside many caves, beautiful, glistening crystal structures hang from the ceilings. They are stalactites – pointed, often huge, natural objects made from minerals contained in dripping rainwater. Some of these icicle-shaped formations can be many thousands of years old! Now you can create a dark and mysterious cave and watch your own stalactites grow day by day.

Dark paint brings a gloomy feel to a home-made cave.

Inside your cave, a solution drips off a string, slowly forming a stalactite.

A CAVE OF YOUR OWN

Most real stalactites form in limestone caves that are made when
underground rivers or rainfall dissolve large spaces in the rock. But
your stalactites will grow perfectly well in a cardboard box — and you
can make them any colour you like, too. You won't beat natural stalactites
for size, though: the world's biggest are several metres long!

You can create
stalactites in any
colour — or add
neon food colouring
to make them glow
under black light!

HOW TO MAKE A
STUNNING STALACTITE

Don't throw away the box those new trainers came in *because* it will make a great cave. To make a stalactite, you need a white mineral powder, magnesium sulfate (commonly called Epsom salt), which most chemists stock. It takes at least a week for a stalactite to form, *so* be patient. And remember: don't put Epsom salt in your mouth, and wash your hands after touching it. The mineral isn't poisonous, but it can upset your stomach.

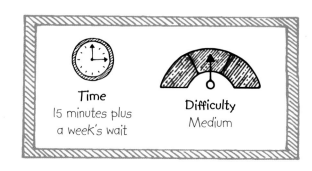

Time
15 minutes plus
a week's wait

Difficulty
Medium

WHAT YOU NEED

Two glasses

Scissors

Plastic cup

Paint

Spoon

String

Paintbrush

Jug of warm water

Epsom salt

Food colouring

Shoe box

1 If the box has an attached lid, cut it off. Then cut out a round hole in the lid – this makes the cave opening. Now trim the lid, so that it fits snugly in the box. Make a note of the side of the box you want to be the top of the cave.

2 Next, make a slit in the top of the box, about 1 cm (⅓ in) wide and 15 cm (6 in) long, though this will depend on the size of your box. Soon, you will make the string dangle through this opening.

3 Paint the box grey to make it look cave-like. If you want to be really geological, paint streaks in other colours to represent minerals in the rocks.

4 Mix the food colouring with the warm water, then pour it into both glasses. Add Epsom salt to both glasses and stir until no more salt will dissolve.

5 Cut off the bottom of the plastic cup to make a shallow bowl. This will catch drips of liquid, as the set up in the next step shows you.

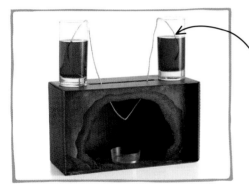

Wet the whole length of the string before you hang it from the glasses.

A stalactite forms slowly where the liquid drips off the string.

6 Cut 40 cm (16 in) of string and put about 10 cm (4 in) of each end in each glass. Place a glass on each end of the box top, with the middle of the string hanging in a "v" shape through the slit.

7 Leave your set up for at least a week: the longer, the better! As the liquid drips off the string, a stalactite will form.

HOW IT WORKS

When the Epsom salt dissolves in the water it breaks down into particles called ions. These mix evenly and invisibly with the water molecules to make a strong solution. The string soaks up the solution all the way along its length through thousands of tiny hollow fibres. When the liquid falls drop by drop, some of the ions in the solution join up, forming a solid crystal, while the water drips away. As more ions join together, the crystal grows.

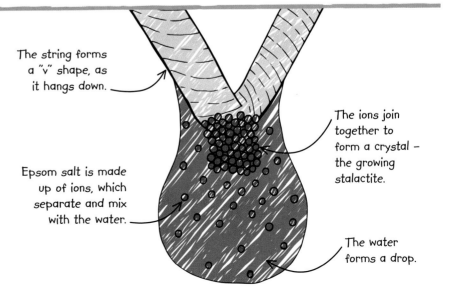

The string forms a "v" shape, as it hangs down.

Epsom salt is made up of ions, which separate and mix with the water.

The ions join together to form a crystal – the growing stalactite.

The water forms a drop.

FIZZING BATH BOMBS

Give your tub the fizz factor with your own fragrant bath bombs. This experiment shows an acid-base reaction, where cream of tartar (an acid) and bicarbonate of soda (a base) dissolve in water to produce soothing, gentle bubbles. Get ready for some serious relaxation.

Your bath bomb begins to dissolve in water.

Food colouring in the bath bomb brightens up your bathwater.

BUBBLY BATH

When your *bath bombs* hit the water, the chemical reaction that takes place releases *bubbles* of carbon dioxide gas. As the bath bombs break up, other things that you put in are released at the same time. This includes food colouring, olive oil, and *essential oils*.

A chemical reaction releases bubbles of carbon dioxide.

HOW TO MAKE
FIZZING BATH BOMBS

To prepare your bath bombs, you need to mix two dry chemicals – cream of tartar and bicarbonate of soda – which react together only once they are immersed in water. Mix them with olive oil to form a moisturizing layer on your skin, a dash of essential oils for a rich fragrance, and food colouring to add some colour.

Time
30 minutes plus two days to dry

Difficulty
Medium

WHAT YOU NEED

Moulds (silicone works best)

Large bowl

150 g (5¼ oz) cream of tartar

Essential oils, such as lavender

300 g (10½ oz) bicarbonate of soda

0.5L

Water in a spray bottle

Two teaspoons olive oil

Teaspoon

Food colouring

Tablespoon

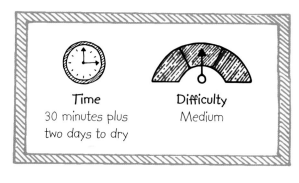

1 Measure the olive oil and pour it into the large bowl. The oil helps to bind the ingredients and, once in the bath, it will moisturize your skin. Add the bicarbonate of soda, cream of tartar, and a few drops of essential oils, such as lavender.

2 Put at least 15 drops of food colouring into the bowl: the colour becomes paler as the powders absorb the food colouring. You'll know this is happening when tiny drops form on the surface.

Mix the dry powders and the wet ingredients together well.

Listen carefully, and you can hear the mixture sizzle.

3 Using a tablespoon, begin to stir all of the ingredients so that everything is well mixed. At this stage, you will notice that the mixture is still quite powdery and that tiny globules of food colouring remain – don't worry, the consistency will change when you add water in the next step.

4 Now add a few sprays of water to the mixture, which will sizzle as the cream of tartar dissolves in the water and begins reacting with the bicarbonate of soda.

Push the mixture into the shape of a cliff – if it crumbles, add a little more water.

Spoon out your mixture into each mould.

Fill up each mould close to the top.

5 The mixture should look and feel less powdery now, and be more like wet sand. Push your spoon into the mixture – if it leaves behind a good shape without crumbling, you are ready to transfer the mixture to the moulds. If necessary, spray some more water and mix again until you get the required consistency.

Put the same amount in each mould.

Leave your bath bombs in their moulds for two days.

Pack the mixture firmly down in the moulds.

6 When you've filled all of the moulds, press hard on the mixture with your fingers. You can also use fingers or a spoon to spread out the powder evenly. The idea is to pack the moulds down firmly and make them as neat as possible.

7 Leave your bath bombs to dry for at least two days. As they lose water to air they will become harder. They won't dry out completely and fall apart because of the olive oil, which keeps the dry powders locked together.

Peel away the moulds gently to avoid breaking the bath bombs.

Don't worry if a bath bomb looks uneven at the surface – it won't have any effect on how well it works.

When an acid and a base react in water, it's called a "neutralization reaction".

8 After a couple of days, gently remove the bath bombs from their moulds. If you are using silicone moulds, you can use them again to make another batch – perhaps using a different colour.

9 They are ready – but remember to keep them away from places where they might get wet... until it's time for a bath, of course!

10 Next time you take a bath, drop in one of your homemade bath bombs and enjoy an invigorating, fizzing sensation. As your bath bomb dissolves and gives off a stream of bubbles, the luxurious moisturizing effect of the olive oil and the calming scent of the essential oils will relax you.

TAKE IT FURTHER

Do you know someone who loves nothing more than to soak in a bath? Fragrant, fizzing, and fun, bath bombs make the perfect gift. You could even add natural ingredients, like dried lavender – or rose petals, shown below. If you want, you can also wrap them up.

1 To make your bath bombs extra special, use dried rose petals – if you can't get them, other dried flowers will work. Mix in the petals as you stir the ingredients together.

2 Then follow the rest of the steps shown in this experiment. When your flowery bath bombs are ready, the rose petals remain trapped inside – until they are released in the bath.

HOW IT WORKS

The fizzing of your bath bombs in water is a sign that a chemical reaction is taking place. The scientific name for bicarbonate of soda – a base – is sodium hydrogen carbonate. It reacts with the acid potassium bitartrate, or cream of tartar, then breaks down into three things: sodium (which dissolves in water), hydroxide (which joins with hydrogen from the acid to make water), and carbon dioxide gas (which forms bubbles).

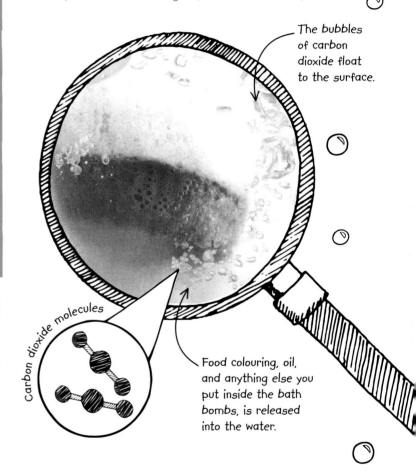

The bubbles of carbon dioxide float to the surface.

Carbon dioxide molecules

Food colouring, oil, and anything else you put inside the bath bombs, is released into the water.

REAL WORLD SCIENCE
FIZZY TABLET

Some vitamin tablets contain a base and an acid that react together when dropped in water. The vitamins are released into a fizzy drink, which is much easier to swallow than dry tablets.

ICY ORBS

It would be easy to mistake these multicoloured, patterned balls for precious jewels, mysterious deep-sea creatures, or even alien worlds from outer space. But actually, they're just balls of coloured ice. No two ice balloons look the same because the food colouring that is added spreads differently through the melted ice of each ball. Remember: they won't last forever, so you might want to photograph your colourful creations before they melt.

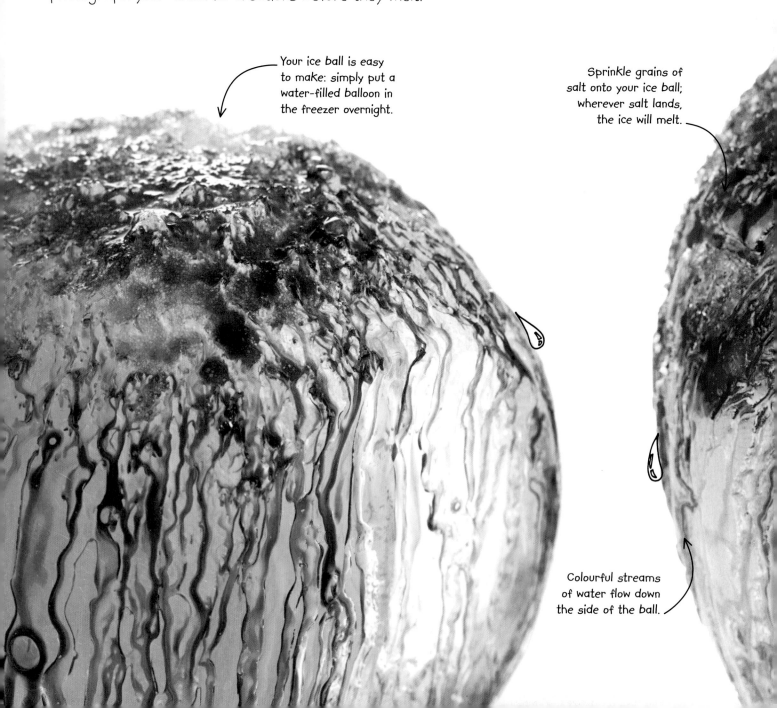

Your ice ball is easy to make: simply put a water-filled balloon in the freezer overnight.

Sprinkle grains of salt onto your ice ball; wherever salt lands, the ice will melt.

Colourful streams of water flow down the side of the ball.

COLOURFUL ICE BALLS

These beautiful balls are made by freezing water in a balloon. Sprinkling salt on top of the ice makes sections of ice melt, creating rivulets of water that run down the sphere's sides. Add food colouring to the mixture and watch it dissolve in the liquid water, making the rivers run green, blue, and any other colour you add, to make pretty patterns.

HOW TO MAKE
ICY ORBS

This simple but effective experiment creates spectacular results: simply make a ball of ice, add salt and food colouring, and watch fabulous patterns paint the ice. You will need to be careful, though; adding salt to ice makes the ice even colder – a mixture of salt and ice can get as cold as -21°C (-6°F), so make sure you don't touch the ice when it is mixed with the salt.

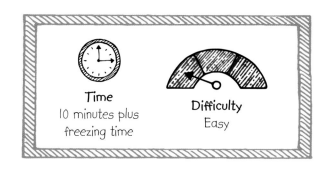

Time
10 minutes plus freezing time

Difficulty
Easy

WHAT YOU NEED

Food colouring (more colours, the better)

Balloon

Large bowl

Salt

Scissors

You will also need a freezer and a water tap

If there is space in your freezer, put the water-filled balloon in a bowl, so it keeps its round shape.

1 Place your balloon's opening over the end of a cold-water tap. Turn the tap to a trickle and half-fill the balloon with water. Remove and tie off the balloon – ask an adult for help if you need it. Put the balloon in the freezer and leave it overnight.

If the ice feels too cold for your hands, wear some gloves.

2 The next day, remove the balloon from the freezer. It should feel hard because the liquid water has turned into solid ice. Cut the tied end off the balloon, and peel off the rubber.

3 Put your ball of ice back in a bowl or on a tray. Sprinkle a little salt on top of the ice ball. Watch the ice melt where the salt grains land, peppering the icy surface with lots of tiny holes.

4 Dribble some food colouring onto the ice. The colouring will mostly sit on top of the solid ice, but it will quickly dissolve in the melted ice to make coloured rivers that stream down the side.

5 To make your icy creation look even more beautiful, add different food colourings. And if you shine the light from a torch or lamp under one of your icy creations, you can get a really spectacular effect!

HOW IT WORKS

Salt grains are crystals, and are made of two types of particle – sodium ions and chloride ions – joined together. When salt is sprinkled on an icy orb, the ions break up the regular arrangement of water molecules in the ice. Once the water molecules are broken apart, the ice becomes liquid. Since sodium and chloride ions attach to the water molecules, the water molecules cannot bond together unless the temperature becomes very cold again.

Salt crystals are made of sodium ions (purple) and chloride ions (green).

This sodium ion breaks apart the ice, turning it into water.

This chloride ion clings to a water molecule (blue) that has broken free.

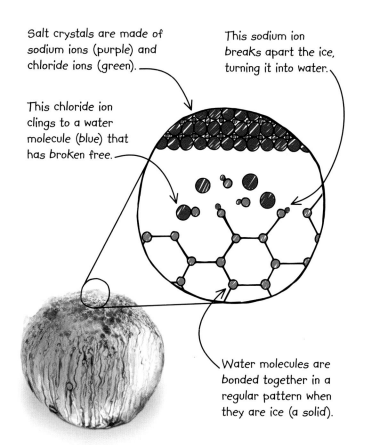

Water molecules are bonded together in a regular pattern when they are ice (a solid).

REAL WORLD SCIENCE
DE-ICING ROADS

In freezing temperatures, specially designed lorries spread salt on major roads and pavements to prevent accidents. The salt melts any snow or ice that is already on these surfaces, and also prevents water from turning into ice. This is because adding salt lowers the freezing point of water.

THE GREAT OUTDOORS

Science can be a breath of fresh air – especially when it takes you outdoors. Here are some projects for creating natural wonders, from your own mini rainforest to an erupting volcano. You can also harness the power of the Sun with just some light-sensitive paper and leaves. Or why not measure the speed of the wind with an effective monitor made mostly out of paper cups? And if you're artistically inclined, there are beautiful things to make and keep.

JUNGLE IN A BOTTLE

In this experiment you'll be making your very own jungle, which will live and grow without needing much help from you. You'll only ever have to water it once. Amazingly, your jungle will then keep itself watered by producing "rain", in much the same way as a real jungle full of thirsty trees does.

SEALED SYSTEM

Although no air or water can get in or out, any plants in the bottle will thrive. They are part of an ecosystem, in which all things in one area – including animals, plants, and even soil – work together for survival.

Your plant needs
sunlight, which
reaches it through
the transparent
plastic bottle.

Water collects
on the inside
of the bottle.

You can add moss
and other small
plants if you like.

The soil holds
water, like
a sponge.

HOW TO MAKE A
JUNGLE IN A BOTTLE

Your little jungle needs a healthy plant potted in clean soil and a 1.5–2 litre (2½–3½ pint) bottle, which you pack with some small stones, pistachio shells, and charcoal. Try to find "activated charcoal", which is extra absorbent. If you can't, just crush up the ordinary kind. Charcoal soaks up chemicals produced by any dead plants and will stop your jungle getting smelly!

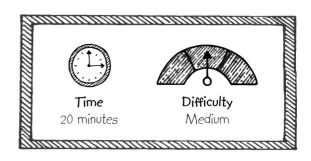

Time
20 minutes

Difficulty
Medium

WHAT YOU NEED

Sticky tape

Pistachio shells

Small stones

Water in a spray bottle

Scissors

Plastic bottle

Crushed charcoal

Potted plant

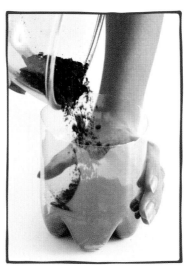

1 Cut the bottle in two, so that the base is about 10 cm (4 in) high. Keep the top part for later. Then put a layer of the small stones into the bottom, and charcoal on top.

2 Pour in the pistachio shells on top of the charcoal. These shells act as a barrier to stop the soil that goes in next from falling into the charcoal and the stones below.

3 Gently take the plant out of its pot and place it on top of the pistachio shells. Try not to shake up the layers when you pick up the bottle.

Be careful of the sharp edge!

4 Add soil from the pot, firmly but gently. Any excess water will drip down through the charcoal, but the stones below will prevent your jungle becoming a soggy bog!

5 Spray the leaves with water, and also pour a little water into the soil to make it damp. Your jungle ecosystem is ready to be closed off from the rest of the world.

6 Now place the top part of the bottle on the base. This is the last time any air or water will get into or out of the bottle. Then seal the join between the two parts of the bottle with sticky tape.

Screw the top on tightly so that no air can get in.

Make sure the join is airtight.

7 Put your jungle somewhere light and warm – but not in direct sunlight. If the bottle gets too warm, the water will evaporate from the bottom of the bottle, rather than passing up through the plant.

HOW IT WORKS

In the natural world, during daytime, water constantly passes through plants in a process called transpiration. The water moves up from the roots and out through tiny holes in the leaves (as invisible vapour). This turns into water droplets that form clouds. In your jungle, the vapour becomes droplets on the inside of the bottle. The water drops onto the soil, like rain, and the cycle begins again.

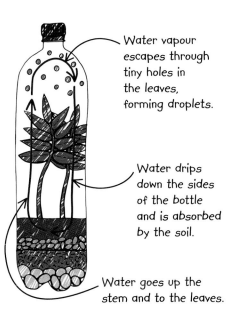

Water vapour escapes through tiny holes in the leaves, forming droplets.

Water drips down the sides of the bottle and is absorbed by the soil.

Water goes up the stem and to the leaves.

REAL WORLD SCIENCE
AMAZON RAINFOREST

The proper term for a jungle is tropical rainforest. Tropical means "near the Equator". These forests are always very misty. Each tree sucks up hundreds of litres of water a day. The air is always full of water vapour – and it rains a lot.

FANTASTIC FOSSILS

We know about the kinds of animals and plants that lived long ago because some of them were preserved as fossils after they died. Real fossils take millions of years to form, but you can make yours in less than 24 hours! Once you've made your fossils, you could bury them in sand and become a fossil hunter... with successful finds guaranteed!

Pick and choose colours that will make your "fozzilized" objects really stand out.

MAKE AN IMPRESSION

The experiment shows you how to make a fossil shell with plaster and then paint it to look incredibly old. But you can use whatever natural object you like as a model. The other "fossil" you see here is a dried starfish. Keep your eyes open when you go to the park or for a walk on a beach. There'll be plenty of things to choose from.

Bury your fake fossils and see if your friends can find them, just like real fossil hunters!

HOW TO MAKE
FANTASTIC FOSSILS

The main ingredient for fossil-making is plaster of Paris. This is a powder that *becomes* a thick liquid when mixed with water, and then sets hard. For safety, find an adult to help you when handling this material. Picking an object that will make a good fossil is the fun part: this can *be* a shell, or anything with an interesting shape and texture.

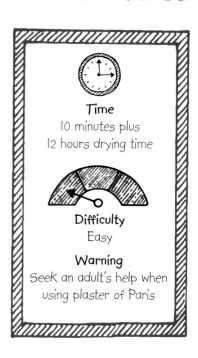

Time
10 minutes plus
12 hours drying time

Difficulty
Easy

Warning
Seek an adult's help when
using plaster of Paris

WHAT YOU NEED

Plastic bowl

Shell

Paint

Plaster of Paris

Modelling clay

Measuring jug filled with water

Spoon

Paintbrush

1 Mix up the plaster of Paris using a little less water than most packets tell you to. One cup of plaster to one cup of water should give you the nice thick liquid you need to work with.

2 Next, line the bottom of the plastic bowl with the modelling clay. You'll need a layer about 2 cm (¾ in) deep. Press the clay down with your fingers to make it as flat as you can.

3 Pick up your shell and press it firmly into the modelling clay. Keep it there for 30 seconds, so it leaves a distinct shape, then remove it carefully. You should see a perfect impression of the shell in the clay.

4 Now pour the plaster of Paris over the shell impression in the clay. Leave it for at least 12 hours, so that it can set hard. Remember: this bit takes thousands or millions of years for a real fossil!

HOW IT WORKS

Your fake fossil most closely resembles a cast fossil. This forms after the soft bits of a plant or an animal rot away, leaving a space that fills with sludge. Over millions of years, the sludge turns into solid rock. Dinosaur experts have found dinosaur footprints preserved this way.

The dinosaur's foot leaves a deep impression.

A dinosaur leaves a footprint in soft waterside mud at low tide.

A fossil hunter chips away the rock and finds the footprint.

As the water rises, sludge fills the footprint, eventually making a rocky cast.

Make sure the plaster has set hard before you paint it.

5 When the plaster is set hard, ease it away from the clay. You can use your fingers to do this, but you may want to use a table knife to lever it out – in which case, ask for an adult to help you. Turn the plaster over and there's your fossil shell.

6 Paint your fossil and the surrounding plaster to make your "find" look real. Try making casts with different objects from around the home – but remember to ask the owner's permission, just in case it is something valuable!

REAL WORLD SCIENCE
FOSSILIZED TRILOBITE

Trilobites were sea creatures that became extinct 250 million years ago. They had a hard outer covering but no internal bones. When their soft inner parts decayed, minerals filled the spaces left behind, and fossils formed.

SHOEBOX PLANT

Plants need food for the same reasons as you do: to stay alive and grow. But, unlike you, plants create their own food, using energy from the Sun. In this experiment, you'll see just how important sunlight is to a plant. You will challenge a bean seedling to find its way through a maze made inside a dark box, following just the tiniest beam of light. It won't take you long to set up the experiment, but you'll have to wait for results. Even the speediest bean needs a few days to grow!

REACHING FOR THE LIGHT

You'll be impressed by the way your plant solves the maze. In its unstoppable search for light, it bends to and fro like a snake as it clambers upwards. This is because the two sides of its stem grow at different rates, depending on the amount of light they receive.

It might take a week or more before you see young, green leaves popping out of the top of your box.

HOW TO MAKE A
SHOEBOX PLANT

This experiment is relatively easy for you – but hard work for the plant! You'll grow a bean from a seed and make a secret obstacle course for it to scramble through. There's some cutting out to do with scissors, but that's the only part you might need help with. You can't start the experiment until your seed produces a shoot. So first pot up your bean and put it on a windowsill for a few days. While you wait, you can build the shoebox maze. Once everything is in place, you'll have to try and be patient for a little longer.

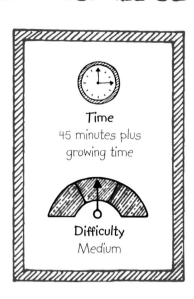

Time
45 minutes plus growing time

Difficulty
Medium

WHAT YOU NEED

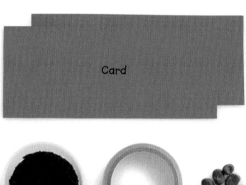

Card

Compost in a plastic cup

Sticky tape

Broad bean seeds

Paints

Paintbrush

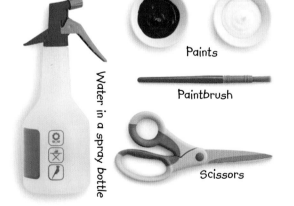

Water in a spray bottle

Scissors

Shoebox

1 Push a broad bean seed into compost, to about 2.5 cm (1 in) below the surface. If you don't have compost, use fine garden soil.

2 Use the water sprayer to dampen the compost – this will make a seed grow in a few days. Make sure it gets sunlight.

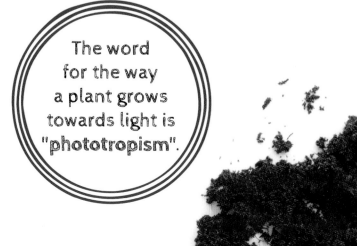

The word for the way a plant grows towards light is "phototropism".

Fold down the ends
of each card to
make flaps.

3 Now get the shoebox and cut a 5 cm (2 in) by 2.5 cm (1 in) hole in the centre of one end. Cover any other holes in the box with tape to stop unwanted light getting through.

4 Paint the box inside and out – this will make it look great when you put it on display. White paint makes a good undercoat, with dark green on top, but you can paint it whatever colour you like.

5 Cut two pieces of card to fit inside the box. Make them wide enough so you can create flaps on both sides. Near the end of each piece of card, cut out a rectangular hole.

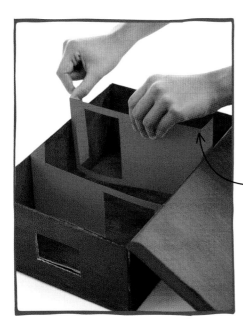

Once a shoot appears, the plant will depend on light to grow.

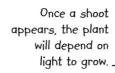

The cards make the maze that your bean seedling will have to find its way through.

6 Use sticky tape to attach the flaps of the cards to the inside of the box. Position one card about one third of the way down the box, and the other about two thirds down. Make sure the two holes are at opposite sides.

7 Meanwhile, check for a green shoot in your cup. Spray on more water if it's too dry. You can start your experiment once the seed has grown, or "germinated", which may take a few days.

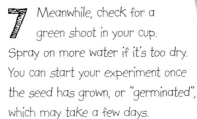

Some light can pass through the hole in the top.

The plant receives only the light that passes through the hole in the bottom card.

8 Place the plastic cup with the compost and your growing plant at the bottom of the box. The mouth of the cup should face outwards, just below the hole in the bottom card.

TAKE IT FURTHER

Now that you have seen how well your plant finds its way through an easy maze, you can set a harder challenge! Try growing a plant through a maze that has smaller holes or an extra piece of card. You could also change other parts of the experiment. What happens if you leave the box open? Will it make a difference if you close off the hole altogether? Can you get a plant to bend without the box, by growing it in a dark place with light coming in from only one direction? You could also use a sprouting potato instead of a bean – no compost or water needed.

Your plant has passed the test and zigzagged through the maze towards the light.

This is what you'll see most of the time, so be patient.

9 Close the box and seal it with tape. Stand it where it won't be toppled over and there is plenty of light. Now and then, unseal the box to water the plant and keep it healthy.

10 Except to water the compost, keep the box closed until you see the tip of the plant's shoot poking through the hole at the top. This might take a week or two, but the end result will be worth the wait!

HOW IT WORKS

Plants use the energy in sunlight to make their own food. In a process called photosynthesis, they soak up the Sun's energy with their leaves and use it to turn water from the soil and carbon dioxide from the air into glucose, a type of sugar. Glucose provides plants with fuel. It is no surprise, then, that plants have evolved a way to grow towards light, so they can sunbathe as much as possible. It's all down to chemicals called auxins. The more auxins in a particular part of the plant, the faster that part will grow. Light destroys auxins, so there will be fewer of them in the side of the stem that receives most light. The shaded side of the plant contains more auxins, so that side grows more quickly. This causes the plant to bend towards the light.

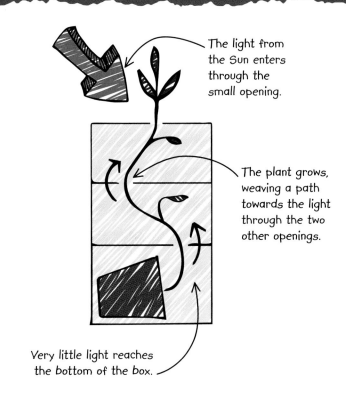

The light from the Sun enters through the small opening.

The plant grows, weaving a path towards the light through the two other openings.

Very little light reaches the bottom of the box.

REAL WORLD SCIENCE
PLANT GROWTH

A young sunflower turns its head from east to west during the day, following the Sun. At night, it turns back to face east again, ready for sunrise the next morning. Both movements are caused by changing levels of auxins inside the plant. Once the sunflower's head has developed, the plant stops following the Sun, usually settling with its head facing east.

PHOTOSYNTHESIS

During daylight, a tree makes glucose by photosynthesis. At night, it uses the nourishing glucose to stay alive and to keep growing.

Sunlight shining on the leaves provides the tree with energy.

The leaves release the oxygen they have made.

The tree takes up carbon dioxide from the air.

The roots spread out to gather a lot of water.

BEAUTIFUL SUN PRINTS

Discover your inner artist by making these intriguing and beautiful Sun prints. You need some special light-sensitive paper, which you can get from most craft shops or online. For best results, do this experiment on a bright sunny day, although it will also work on a cloudy day – it just takes a little longer. You can use any flat or nearly flat objects, such as leaves and feathers, to create a stunning gallery.

Think about what shape of frame works best with your Sun print – square, rectangle, or something else entirely.

Light-sensitive paper reacts to sunlight to create the wonderful deep blue shade of a Sun print.

BLUE-AND-WHITE ART

You will be able to make only blue and white images. The white areas in these prints are actually the shadows of the objects used. For the most striking effects, you could frame your artistic creations and display them on the wall. You can cut a simple shape frame out of cardboard, but to show off a real masterpiece you might want to add a ready-made wooden frame as well.

A circular card mount gives a "designer touch" to the Sun print of this fern.

HOW TO MAKE
BEAUTIFUL SUN PRINTS

This experiment uses light-sensitive paper, which is coated with chemicals that react to sunlight. For best results, pick a sunny day and work outside. Remember, this is a fast-paced project, so have a tray of water ready to immerse the paper when the exposure time is up. Once exposed to light, you can't use this paper again.

Time
10 minutes plus a few hours waiting time

Difficulty
Easy

WHAT YOU NEED

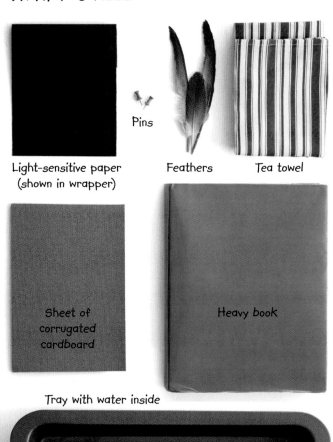

Light-sensitive paper
(shown in wrapper)

Pins

Feathers

Tea towel

Sheet of corrugated cardboard

Heavy book

Tray with water inside

1 Go outside and take one sheet of the light-sensitive paper out of its pack. Then, pin it to the cardboard sheet and, as fast as possible, arrange the feathers on the paper. Wait for a few minutes and try not to move anything.

2 The paper will turn from deep blue to pale blue. Then, remove the feathers and unpin the paper from the card. You'll see shadows where the feathers stopped the sunlight from reaching the paper.

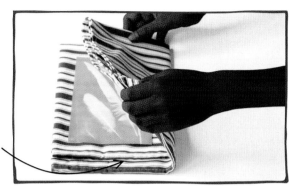

Use a tea towel to soak up water from the wet paper.

3 As quickly as you can, immerse the paper in the tray of water. You'll notice that the deep blue colour of the feathers washes right off, and the pale blue areas turn darker blue. Leave the paper in the water for a few minutes.

4 To dry the paper, place it carefully in a clean, folded tea towel. Then put a heavy book on top of the tea towel, as this will help press out the water and keep the paper flat. Leave the paper pressed inside the towel for at least a few hours.

5 Unfold the tea towel to check the paper. If it's dry, your Sun print is ready! You will see how the paper has changed colour yet again. The blue areas are much darker now, so the white feather prints really stand out.

Ultraviolet light from the Sun causes the compound Prussian blue to form.

Marvel at the stunning detail of the feather prints.

TAKE IT FURTHER

Why not show off your beautiful Sun prints to your friends and family in a sophisticated frame? All you need is a ruler, pencil, piece of card, glue, and scissors.

1 Using a ruler and sharp pencil, draw a rectangle on a thick piece of card. Make the rectangle slightly smaller than the Sun print paper. Cut it out carefully.

2 Spread a generous amount of glue around the back of the frame, then stick on the Sun print paper. Make sure you place it the right way up!

HOW IT WORKS

Light-sensitive paper is coated in chemicals that react together when they are exposed to a type of light called ultraviolet. This reaction causes a deep-blue compound, known as Prussian blue, to form on the paper. When the paper is put in water, the original chemicals – which remain in areas that sunlight hasn't reached – wash away, but Prussian blue stays on the paper.

REAL WORLD SCIENCE
FRAGILE FLAG

If some materials are left in sunlight for a long time, ultraviolet light can damage them. So important museum objects, like this 200-year-old American flag, are often kept in dimly lit areas.

ERUPTING VOLCANO

Volcanoes are huge cone-shaped mountains formed over thousands, or millions, of years. Every so often they erupt, sending hot, melted liquid rock out of the top of the cone, called the crater. Now you can make your own volcano to dominate landscape, being a plastic bottle and thick paste, and let rip with a spectacular eruption!

The land around
a real volcano
sometimes floods
with molten lava.

LAVA FLOW

HOW TO MAKE AN
ERUPTING VOLCANO

This gets messy, so work outdoors if you can. Your volcano is built from papier mâché, made from newspaper dunked in a runny paste. The spectacular eruption is produced by two very ordinary household products: vinegar and bicarbonate of soda. If you clean and dry the volcano with kitchen paper or tissues after an eruption, you can use it again and again.

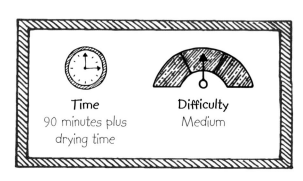

Time
90 minutes plus drying time

Difficulty
Medium

WHAT YOU NEED

Bicarbonate of soda   Vinegar   Warm water   Washing-up liquid

400 g (14 oz) flour   Bowl of water

Large piece of cardboard

Newspaper   Small plastic bottle

Paintbrush

Packing tape   Spoon   Paints

Scissors   Food colouring

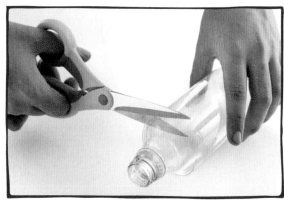

1 Using your scissors, carefully cut off the top of the bottle. This is so you can easily add the ingredients later on – and for it to come out again in the form of an eruption. This will be the centre of the volcano, with the bottle's mouth as the crater.

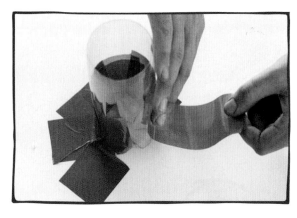

2 Using several pieces of packing tape, stick the bottle to the middle of your large piece of cardboard. When everything is secure, you're ready to start building up the volcano's cone around the bottle.

Pull the tape tight so that the paper balls can't move.

3 Tear off several pieces of newspaper and scrunch them into tight balls. Arrange the paper balls around the bottle. Make the stack wider at the bottom than at the top. Tape the balls securely to the cardboard base and to the bottle.

4 Now you can shape the volcano's cone using papier mâché. To begin with, tear or cut 50 or more strips of newspaper, about 2–3 cm (¾–1¼ in) wide. These will be dunked in a watery glue, which you make from flour and water in step 5.

Add the flour just a small amount at a time.

Overlap the strips in a way to create your desired shape.

5 To make the glue, add flour to the bowl of water and mix it in with a spoon. Keep on adding flour and mixing until you have a runny paste about as thick as pancake batter. Note, you might not need all the flour.

6 Saturate the newspaper strips in the paste. Run the strips through your fingers to remove excess paste, then lay them over the paper cone. Smooth out the strips, sticking some to the cardboard base and over the mouth of the bottle.

7 You've now built your volcano's cone. The papier mâché must dry and harden before you go on to the next stage. So leave it in a warm place overnight.

When the papier mâché is dry, it's time to paint it.

The cone of a **real volcano** is made of old lava that has **cooled** and **turned solid**.

Stand your volcano somewhere warm, so the paint dries quickly.

8 Paint the cone dark brown, but leave an unpainted strip at the bottom. If you don't have brown paint, mix together red, green, and blue. If you can get it, add a little sand for a gritty texture.

9 Paint the bottom of the cone and the cardboard base in shades of green to represent the grass or jungle below. If you like, paint the top of the cone red, to look like fiery lava.

10 Here comes the really messy bit! Pour the ingredients shown below into the volcano's opening. Once you have added them all, mix them with a spoon.

11 Get your camera out if you have one because your volcano is about to explode! Add two or three teaspoons of bicarbonate of soda into the volcano's cone and wait for a few seconds.

The mixture bubbles up to the top of the cone.

A foamy liquid spills over and pours down the slopes, just like real lava in a volcanic eruption.

Pour in about 40 ml (1½ fl oz) of washing-up liquid.

Pour in about 40 ml (1½ fl oz) of warm water.

Pour in about 50 ml (1¾ fl oz) of vinegar.

Finally, add a few drops of red food colouring.

TAKE IT FURTHER

Instead of using papier mâché on a cardboard base, you could use mud to build up a volcano cone on a wooden base. In this version, just leave a hole in the top of the soil cone and press a plastic cup into it. This makes the crater where you will mix up the lava. If you're allowed to use lots of vinegar and bicarbonate of soda, stir up a really large cupful of ingredients and create a truly gigantic eruption. Or you could see what happens if you replace bicarbonate of soda with cola, which contains phosphoric acid.

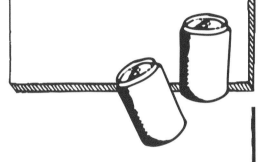

HOW IT WORKS

Mixing bicarbonate of soda (a base) with vinegar (which contains acetic acid) causes a rapid chemical reaction that produces lots of carbon dioxide gas. Tiny bubbles of this gas become trapped in the washing-up liquid in your lava mixture. This creates a foam that takes up much more space than the liquid ingredients – so it all comes frothing out of the mouth of the volcano and trickles down the sides. Real lava has tiny bubbles of carbon dioxide in it, too. When it cools and sets hard, the bubbles are trapped.

REAL WORLD SCIENCE
TUNGARAHUA VOLCANO

Your volcano is the shape of what is known as a cinder cone volcano. Tungarahua, shown in the picture, is an active volcano of this type in Ecuador, South America. When it erupts, lava and ash run down and solidify, forming another layer of rock to build up the growing cone.

INSIDE A VOLCANO

There are several types of volcano, but deep inside each one there is a large pool of molten rock, called the magma chamber. When underground pressures increase, the magma is pushed into a central tube and out through the crater as lava.

When the flow starts to slow, keep the fun going by adding more bicarbonate of soda and vinegar.

Red food colouring makes your foamy mixture actually look like lava.

The lava is easy to wipe up when the eruption is finally over.

The cone is made up of many layers of solidified lava.

When the volcano isn't erupting, the magma remains in the chamber.

An erupting volcano releases huge amounts of smoke and ash, as well as lava.

Lava runs out from the crater and spills down the sides of the cone.

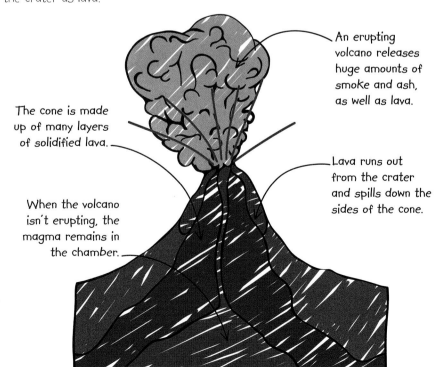

WIND CATCHER

Find out how to read the wind! The only difference between a howling gale and a gentle breeze is how fast the air is going. Meteorologists, the people who study weather, use a device called an anemometer to measure wind speed. You can easily make one of these for yourself – and then broadcast weather reports to your family or your class at school! There are different kinds of anemometer, but lots of them have several cups to catch the wind – just like the model shown here.

As the wind catches the cups, it pushes the anemometer around.

MEASURING THE WIND

This type of anemometer, called a Robinson anemometer, has cups that go whizzing round and round when they catch the wind. At a weather station, a sensor automatically measures the speed of rotation. But with your anemometer, which is made with paper cups, you do the counting yourself.

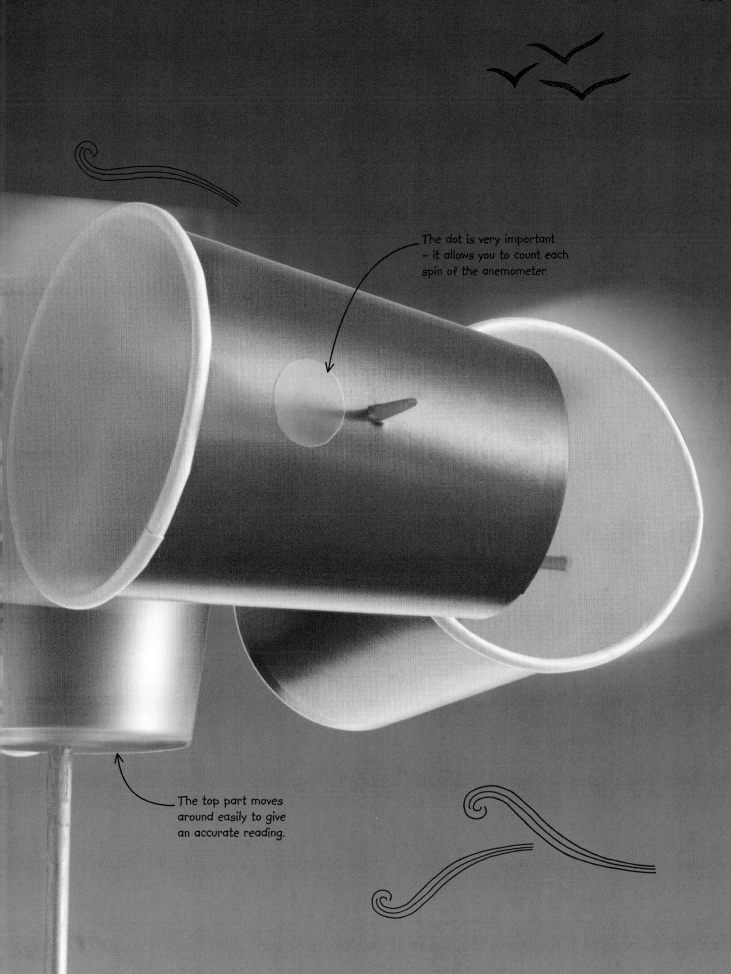

The dot is very important – it allows you to count each spin of the anemometer.

The top part moves around easily to give an accurate reading.

HOW TO MAKE A
WIND CATCHER

For your anemometer to work properly, you must make sure it can't wobble. Either fix it to a table or on top of a wall with adhesive putty, or just hold it in your hand. Find a nice breezy place to conduct your experiment – a sheltered spot won't do! Count how many times the cups spin in one minute, by watching a specially marked cup. Note the number of spins on different days and in different sites.

Time
20 minutes

Difficulty
Medium

WHAT YOU NEED

Six paper cups

Wooden skewers

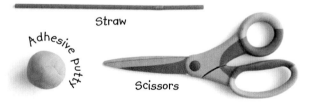

Straw

Adhesive putty

Scissors

Tape

Card

1 Cut the straw to a length of about 10 cm (4 in). If it's a bendy straw, just snip off the bendy bit. Then use the scissors to split one end of the straw into four flaps, each about 2 cm (¾ in) long.

2 Open out the straw flaps. Then, using a few blobs of adhesive putty, fix the flaps onto the bottom of an upturned paper cup. Stand the straw up as straight as possible. In your finished anemometer, this cup will be the other way up.

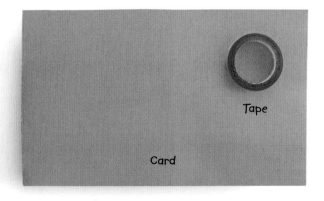

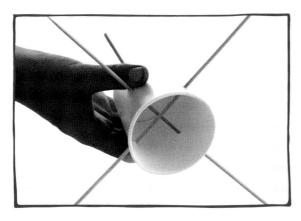

Turn the four cups until they all face the same way.

3 Push a skewer right through the cup with the attached straw – mind your fingers on the sharp ends! Do the same with a second skewer, placing it at right angles to the first one.

4 Use the third skewer to pierce holes through the middles of four more cups. These cups will slot on to the two skewers sticking out of the middle cup. Push them into place.

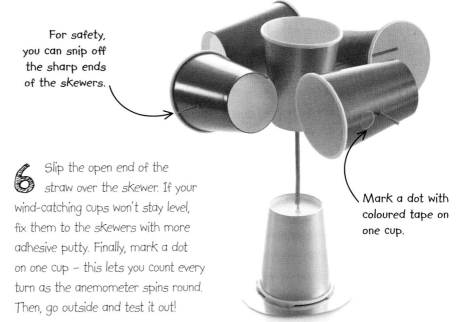

For safety, you can snip off the sharp ends of the skewers.

6 Slip the open end of the straw over the skewer. If your wind-catching cups won't stay level, fix them to the skewers with more adhesive putty. Finally, mark a dot on one cup – this lets you count every turn as the anemometer spins round. Then, go outside and test it out!

Mark a dot with coloured tape on one cup.

5 Cut out a card circle and press a lump of adhesive putty on to it. Push the skewer through the final cup and press the skewer and cup rim into the putty.

HOW IT WORKS

As the wind blows, it pushes the mouth of one cup and also the base of the cup on the opposite end of the same skewer. The force is greater on the cup with its mouth facing into the wind, so the anemometer will spin. This brings the other pair of cups into the wind. The faster the wind blows, the more times the cups rotate per minute.

REAL WORLD SCIENCE
WIND TURBINE

Wind can be very powerful, supplying enough energy to turn massive wind turbines. These, in turn, drive electric generators, so the energy ends up as electricity used to power homes, schools, offices, and factories. If the wind speed doubles, the energy increases not twice as much – but an amazing eight times as much!

GLOSSARY

ACID
A substance that when dissolved in water produces positively charged ions of hydrogen. Lemon juice and vinegar are examples of acids.

AIR RESISTANCE
A force that acts on an object moving through air, in the opposite direction to the object's motion.

ATOM
The smallest part of an element.

ATTRACTION
A force that pulls things together.

BACTERIA
Microscopic, single-celled organisms. Some can cause illness, but most are harmless.

BASE
A kind of substance that reacts with an acid to give water and salt.

BOND
A force that holds together tiny particles such as atoms and molecules.

CARBON DIOXIDE
A compound found as a gas in the air all around us. We breathe out carbon dioxide as a waste product.

CELL
1. The smallest living part of a living thing. Plants and animals are made of up to trillions of cells. 2. A chemical device that forms part of an electric battery.

CELLULOSE
A compound that forms the tough fibres of plant cell walls.

CHEMICAL
A compound or element that can change when combined with another substance. Chemicals can be liquids, solids, or gases.

CIRCUIT
A complete and closed path, around which an electric current can flow.

COMPOUND
A chemical made of two or more elements. For example, water is a compound, made of the elements hydrogen and oxygen.

COMPRESSION
A squashing force, such as that experienced by weight-bearing materials in buildings.

CONDUCTOR
A substance through which heat or electricity can easily pass.

CRYSTAL
A regular arrangment of atoms or molecules held together by bonds in a solid.

DENSITY
The amount of mass there is in a particular volume.

DNA
Short for "deoxyribonucleic acid". DNA is a compound found in the cells of all living things. DNA holds coded instructions (genes) that control what people, animals, and plants look like and how they function.

ELECTRIC CURRENT
Movement of electric charge.

ELECTRON
A tiny particle in an atom that has a negative electric charge.

ELEMENT
A substance made of just one type of atom that cannot be broken down into a simpler substance by chemical reactions.

ENERGY
The ability to make things happen. Energy has different forms, such as electrical energy and kinetic energy (movement).

EVAPORATION
The process by which a liquid turns into a gas, usually because of an increase in temperature.

FILTRATION
The process of separating solids from liquids by passing the mixture through a filter.

FOSSIL
The remains or traces of a long-dead animal or plant that have been preserved in rock.

GENE
Part of the DNA found in every living cell. Genes help to make living things the way they are, such as a tall, brown-eyed person or a leafy plant.

GENOME
The complete set of information carried by all the genes in a living thing. The human genome consists of about 20,000 genes.

GLUCOSE
A compound made by plants during photosynthesis. Glucose is a sugar, and is used for energy.

GRAVITY
An attractive force between two objects. Gravity keeps you on the ground instead of floating around.

HELIX
A shape that winds round like a spiral staircase. DNA molecules have a double helix shape.

INSULATOR
A substance through which heat or electricity cannot pass easily.

ION
An atom that has gained or lost electrons, so gaining a negative or positive electric charge.

LED
Short for "light-emitting diode". An LED is an electronic component that lights up when an electric current flows through it.

MASS
A measure of the amount of matter in an object.

MATTER
The name used for the materials that make up the Universe.

MICRO-ORGANISM
Any microscopic thing that is alive, such as bacteria.

MINERAL
A natural material, normally found underground. There are hundreds of different types. Rocks are made of minerals.

MIXTURE
A substance made of two or more compounds or elements.

MOLECULE
Two or more atoms held together by bonds.

NEUTRON
A tiny particle in an atom that contains no electric charge.

NON-NEWTONIAN FLUID
A liquid that can change its form and behaviour depending upon the forces applied to it.

ORBIT
The path of a planet, comet, or asteroid through space around the Sun, or the path of a moon around a planet. Gravity keeps objects in orbit.

OXYGEN
An element. One of the gases in air, essential for most of the life on Earth.

PHOTOSYNTHESIS
The process by which green plants make food from carbon dioxide and water using the energy of the Sun.

PHOTOTROPISM
The way a plant turns and bends towards the sunlight.

PRESSURE
A force applied to a surface, particularly by gases or liquids.

PROTEIN
A particular type of compound essential to life. Proteins make up skin and hair, and also carry out all sorts of functions that keep you alive.

PROTON
A tiny particle in an atom that carries a positive electric charge.

REPULSION
A force that pushes things away from each other.

SOLUTION
A mixture of two chemicals, normally a solid dissolved into a liquid.

STALACTITE
An icicle-like structure hanging from a cave roof, formed gradually from minerals deposited by dripping water.

STALAGMITE
A column rising from the floor of a cave, formed gradually from minerals deposited by dripping water.

STATIC ELECTRICITY
The build-up of electric charge on an object that has lost or gained electrons.

STREAMLINED
An object shaped in a way that offers very little resistance to the flow of liquid or gas.

SUGAR
One of many sweet-tasting compounds, such as glucose.

SURFACE TENSION
A force that pulls the surface of a liquid tight. It is the result of attraction between atoms or molecules.

TENSION
A pulling force, such as that exerted by the steel cables used in parts of buildings or bridges.

TRANSPIRATION
The movement of water through the tubes in a plant's stem and leaves and its evaporation as vapour through tiny holes in the leaves.

ULTRAVIOLET RADIATION (UV)
A form of radiation. A type of light that's invisible to human eyes.

VAPOUR
A gas that easily changes into a liquid if it is cooled or put under pressure.

VIRUS
A non-living microscopic particle, smaller than a cell. Viruses reproduce by invading living cells, and can cause illness.

VISCOSITY
The resistance of a liquid to changing shape. A thick, sticky substance like honey flows slowly because it has a high viscosity.

VOLTAGE
A measure of the force that pushes electrons around a circuit.

VOLUME
The size of a three-dimensional space occupied by something or enclosing something.

INDEX

ACKNOWLEDGMENTS

The publisher would like to thank the following people for their assistance in the preparation of this book:
NandKishor Acharya, Rajesh Singh Adhikari, Shahid Mahmood, Mary Sandberg, and Sachin Singh for design assistance; Steve Crozier and Phil Fitzgerald for retouching; Niki Dirnberger for editorial assistance; Sean Ross for illustrations and testing the experiments; Edwood Burn for illustration assistance; Jackie Brind for indexing; Ruth O'Rourke for proofreading; Laura Gardner, Tessa Jordens, and Max Moore for hand modelling; Lorna Rhodes, home economist, for her help with the baked Alaska experiment; Dan Gardner for testing assistance.

The publisher would like to thank the following for their kind permission to reproduce their photographs:

(Key: a-above; b-below/bottom; c-centre; f-far; l-left; r-right; t-top)

13 Alamy Images: Simon Perkin (br). 23 Getty Images: ra-photos / E+ (bl). 27 Getty Images: Imstepf Studios Llc / DigitalVision (cb). 33 Corbis: Ashley Cooper / Terra (br). 43 Getty Images: Andrew Brookes (br). 49 Dreamstime.com: Bob Phillips - Digital69 (br). 55 Dreamstime.com: Katja Nykanen - Catyamaria (br). 73 Getty Images: CT757fan / E+ (crb). 77 Alamy Images: Travelscape Images (crb). 91 Dreamstime.com: Monthian Ritchan-ad - Thailoei92 (cb). 97 Getty Images: Doug Armand / Photographer's Choice (crb).

103 Getty Images: LatitudeStock - Emma Durnford / Gallo Images (crb). 107 Dreamstime.com: Ivangelos (bc). 113 Getty Images: Geraldo Caso / AFP (clb). 123 Science Photo Library: Martyn F. Chillmaid (bc). 127 Dreamstime.com: Buurserstraat386 (bc). 133 Alamy Images: Mint Images - Frans Lanting (crb). 137 Getty Images: National Geographic Magazines (crb). 143 Dreamstime. com: Lyudmila6304 (clb). 147 Press Association Images: Pablo Martinez Monsivais / AP (bc). 153 Getty Images: Sebastián Crespo Photography (ca). 157 Alamy Images: Ryan McGinnis (bc).

All other images © Dorling Kindersley
For further information see: www.dkimages.com